Beverley Charles grew up and was educated in Yorkshire. His one great ambition in those days was to become a professional footballer, but after leaving school, he managed to arrange a trial at Hull City AFC. But Beverley failed to make the grade and so drifted in and out of dull jobs until he got the opportunity to travel to Africa where Beverley opened his own clothing business. He has four children and now lives in London.

This book is dedicated to my children James, Alexandra Samantha and Atieno.

Beverley Charles Foster

THE RELUCTANT OUTSIDER

AUSTIN MACAULEY PUBLISHERS
LONDON * CAMBRIDGE * NEW YORK * SHARJAH

Copyright © Beverley Charles Foster 2024

The right of Beverley Charles Foster to be identified as the author of this work has been asserted by the author in accordance with sections 77 and 78 of the Copyright, Designs and Patents Act 1988.

All rights reserved. No part of this publication may be reproduced, stored in a retrieval system, or transmitted in any form or by any means, electronic, mechanical, photocopying, recording, or otherwise, without the prior permission of the publishers.

Any person who commits any unauthorised act in relation to this publication may be liable to criminal prosecution and civil claims for damages.

The story, experiences, and words are the author's alone.

A CIP catalogue record for this title is available from the British Library.

ISBN 9781398494831 (Paperback)
ISBN 9781398494848 (ePub e-book)

www.austinmacauley.com

First Published 2024
Austin Macauley Publishers Ltd®
1 Canada Square
Canary Wharf
London
E14 5AA

Throughout my time I have been privileged to encounter some great men and women either in person or by picking up their books. They have inspired me to write this memoir because of their knowledge and wisdom. However, I also learnt from them that for every certainty the opposite is also possible.

Table of Contents

Chapter 1: The Return	11
Chapter 2: New Beginning	19
Chapter 3: Breaking Free	30
Chapter 4: The Seeker	37
Chapter 5: Out of Body	44
Chapter 6: Initiation into Another Reality	54
Chapter 7: New Wine	62
Chapter 8: The Dark Side	71
Chapter 9: Moving On	74
Chapter 10: Who Am I?	82
Chapter 11: Future Islands	89
Chapter 12: The Wisdom of Insecurity	106
Chapter 13: Slums and Slumlords	116
Chapter 14: Dark Night of the Soul	124
Chapter 15: Letting Go	133
Chapter 16: Homeless, Not Hopeless	144

Chapter 1
The Return

My name is George Dexton, and I'm returning home from a self-imposed exile. I've been travelling on a journey through life that has kept me away for 32 years, from the people and places that remember me. The time has come to return not because it was neatly planned or by desire, but by fate, if you believe in that. I did not imagine there would be a time to return; it just turned out that way, mostly because of an incident that happened on the islands where I was located, which was now causing people to become extremely ill and some had died from drinking contaminated tap water.

I had been working in the city of Murgone on the main island of this southern hemisphere archipelago in the middle of the vast ocean. It is most popularly known as the 'Future Islands', probably because it feels like you entered a time warp when you first visit here, with its advanced holistic lifestyle that seems to enlighten all the senses and liberate the soul. The people who live here tend to be either soul seekers or people with varying degrees of curiosity about the prospects of evolution and their part in it.

I had been working on the islands in a busy hotel when this disaster struck without much warning. I had arrived at work on the Monday morning only to find the offices empty. The company had closed its doors without warning. They had forgotten to inform me that they were forced to close due to the report of a mysterious poisonous substance that had been found in the island's water supply.

This had started out a few weeks ago as a rumour, but now it had been reported that a few people had been rushed to the emergency ward of the main hospital in a serious condition, also with some fatalities. The one unusual thing about this tragedy was that it was believed to only affect visitors to the islands, and all of the locals seemed to be immune to this sudden occurrence.

So, with the day off, I wandered through the inner-city streets down by the main piazza, but this time there was an eerie silence about this once thriving tourist attraction, now without the buzzing crowds. However, there was the odd person milling around in silence, almost peaceful. Then a busker started playing, and it echoed around the huge empty square and the tall whitewashed buildings. They must have forgotten to inform him too! Most of the massive cruiser ships in the harbour were now stood silent and devoid of life on board as they had been grounded due to the cancellations from fearful visitors.

After enjoying the unusually serene atmosphere, I wandered into a sparsely filled café to grab a lonely coffee before heading home. No germs can survive boiled water, so I felt confident in the purity of the coffee. My job has been put on hold for an indefinite time, so I have decided to take a break from the islands and head north, following my instincts like a bird beginning its migration route home.

Maybe my days of living on the island are numbered, and new experiences are on the horizon. That's when it hits me that the direction I'm actually heading is on my way to my ancestral 'home' after being absent all this time from the roots of my childhood for over 30 years. I had thought that I hadn't really missed the place that much, but now I know I was probably trying not to let these feelings of nostalgia enter my psyche and cause me to reminisce about the past because it may bring up some regrets about how I lived my life as a young and selfish adolescent who didn't seem to have a thought in his head about anyone else, let alone my own well-being. I suppose it takes time for some lessons to be learnt, and as William Blake noted that, 'An error often has to run its full course before it can be corrected'. It can take a whole lifetime to learn one lesson in life. In fact, most of us will spend far more time and money on a destructive life style of overindulgence than on the growth of self-development.

The flights out of the islands are fully booked for days, so I have decided to take one of the few ships leaving. There are lots of people leaving on the ship that heads towards the northern hemisphere, but the rumbling of the engine is the only sound as people are in a subdued disbelief of the reality of what is going on, now that they are forced out of their busy lifestyles. There is a strange hushed silence as though being in a library. The atmosphere is surreal, like it was some kind of scene from a distant future in a sci-fi movie, as the reality has not fully hit home yet.

Eventually, after arriving in London, I now find myself heading north on the homeward bound bus with crowds of people around me, and having to listen to all their gory details of their hectic lives and what they did the night before. I sometimes wish I could have been a bit more brazen like some of them when I'm around strangers. It's one of the characteristics of the people around these parts. They are down-to-earth and open. 'There's now as queer as folk' as they say in Yorkshire.

The landscape turns greener and the air fresher the further we get into the northern parts of England. Then there is the familiar smell of fish as we arrive in the city of Hull with its unique white telephone boxes sparsely placed among the terraced red-brick houses and corner shops, which are all a comforting reminder of a place that was once a safe and happy haven as a child. I remember all the enthusiasm and excitement of youth as I rushed around not even thinking about the past or the future. Now I am a little more subdued and pensive from a life of ups and downs after I had left this place in search of greater adventure. So it is strange to be back and reflecting on what seems like a 'past life'.

Upon arriving, I realise I'm woven into the fabric of the place like a single red thread running through a huge tapestry that is affected by and affects the whole. I'm interconnected to the people here in a greater oneness. There is a deep connection because it was here that I first began to experience interacting with people from outside my immediate family and first developed the awe of intimacy with strangers, both male and female, in adolescence that so intrigued me. The laughs, the joys, the loves, and the inevitable hurt from learning how to manoeuvre in the big wide world.

The memories come flooding back in waves that wash over my mind like it was yesterday and most of the places still look the same. Many of the experiences have gone forever from my mind just as some of the places have been bulldozed from the scenery without trace, rubbed out like a large eraser on a pencil drawing. I'm seeing the place now from a new perspective, like I was an intruder or a foreign visitor, without prejudice but just as the observer or the overseer. I feel like a ruler over his land, and yet nobody knows who I am.

I feel I belong here, but I don't, because there is a new generation that has emerged over time and has left me estranged from the crowds. There are still a few cousins of mine who live here and a few old friends that I know of. I haven't informed any of them that I'm back because I came on the spur of the moment. I'm sure I would recognise some of the old faces in the streets if I saw them because I have a memory for faces and old souls that I once knew. Anyhow, it's a big city, and the odds of a chance meeting are rare.

I've booked in for a three-month stay just to get a break from the islands and try to reflect on what has really happened over the years since I departed on this epic journey. I have been a wanderer in all those years, and I feel now like the prodigal son who has finally given in to a life on the run, always searching for my 'Self', I suppose. Some would probably say, 'to get away from myself'! I haven't come back with any great fanfare or wealth to share but just a little more matured, and I have developed new dimensions of my old self in this world of multi-dimensional possibilities. I haven't even come back to a welcome with a feast of fatted calves and music playing like in the biblical return. I just drifted in unannounced and unnoticed, almost like the day I departed.

I will spare you most of the details of my childhood here, but just to say that I was a shy, sensitive child who was easily influenced by the more extroverted and daring kids, and therefore I got into a lot of scrapes and sticky situations that I struggled to get out of. Leaving was then probably a quest to find the real me behind a once shaky and fragile personality. I remember now that leaving was a confusing time for me because I really didn't want to let go of the comforting happy times and the good friends and lovers in my life. Change is always met with resistance, and I tried to find all sorts of excuses not to go.

Like finding a better job or meeting the true love of my life, but it was not to be, as I knew instinctively that I was not ready to settle down like so many of my friends who had found their chosen careers and were looking to get mortgages to buy a 'two up, two down', in the suburbs and settle down with someone of marriage material and the sense of certainty of a secure future. This was not for me. I knew I had something to do, somewhere to go, someone to be; besides, I had already left in my mind, long before the physical event of departure had wrenched me away from the only place I really knew. I had known that my time here was up and I had to go.

If I stayed any longer I might die this way and miss my chance of liberation. I knew there was a lesson in there somewhere. I must have been in survival mode when I fled because leaving was the very thing that had saved me from sinking into 'somnambulism' and a futile existence. I had been drifting in and out of menial jobs and even spent some time on the dole, which reduced me to depression and the feeling of being like a parasite living off others. My life had become one-dimensional, like living in a straight line!

I had reached my 27th birthday and remembered the many wandering souls who had joined the '27 club' and committed suicide. For me, it wasn't so dramatic, but I was at a crucial crossroads in my life that led to much confusion and searching because I had not found a direction nor a purpose that I could confidently say 'that this is me and this is what I want to do!'. I had experienced many different jobs and relationships. I spent tough times unemployed with very little money due to the recession during the Thatcher Government of the eighties.

It may have been a depressing time to be around in those dark days, but my disillusionment was deeper than just a passing trend. You see, I always had the inability to fully fit in with the enthusiasm of the kids I grew up with. It's not that I didn't have any friends at school or that I was a loner, but more that I was convinced this was not how life was meant to be. There was a niggling dissatisfaction about my lot. I could not grasp the moment fully, as if there was something missing. I felt like a foreigner in my own culture. I felt like Albert Camus's *Outsider*, searching for meaning in a futile world.

As the last few days grew closer, I could feel the mixed emotions of fear and excitement swirling around in my mind as I tried to find some reason to reassure myself that I wasn't getting carried away by my desire to be in a state of constant movement like a fresh flowing river. 'Treading water feels like drowning', to me at any rate and if 'Patience is a virtue' then I had not learnt this simple lesson of life yet, for it only seemed to apply to the elders in society who were winding down and preparing for their inevitable demise.

I could feel a constant tugging of my desire to seek something that I had never quite put my finger on. Like there was a purpose to my life and I knew there was something out there for me that I could finally grasp, but to know the future would of course take away the newness of life and render me incapable of any spontaneity derived from anticipation. Maybe it's justification I'm looking for because if I was to be honest with myself I know this constant restlessness could be escapism. I recognised the signs of an addiction here because these cravings of being in flight and constant movement come from a fear of commitment, routine, and confinement. I needed to move in order to breathe.

So, I took the plunge into the abyss knowing that, 'the journey of a thousand miles begins with the first step'. I have youth on my side and that meant I had just a little fear of the unknown and in fact the fear of the future is what seems to be driving me forward. It's that sense of adventure that all the great explorers of the past must have been driven on by. I know there are very few places on earth that have not been discovered, but it's not so much the physical adventure that I seek.

It's more the unknown corridors of the psyche that intrigue me and for some reason it is the 'mystique' of Africa that has caught my imagination. I'm drawn by the 'chaotic' flavour of spontaneity and the fear of uncertainty that's in the air. The English philosopher, Colin Wilson states, "The only way to deal with chaos, is deeper into chaos. Adventure is surely the conquering of chaos caused by fear! There is an inner drive or intuition that grows until we lose our moorings and, with some anxiety and concern, we nevertheless leave for good."

Excited and scared I wandered if the plan was brilliant or stupid but at least I had a sense that the universe was a good place and so like the young fledglings about to take their first flight from their nest, I too have reached the 'point of no return' and so boarded my plane out of here!

Chapter 2
New Beginning

"I shall be gone and live or stay and die"
by Shakespeare.

I had arrived at Johannesburg international airport in mid-July. The sun is bright and the runway is dancing with mirages, even though in the southern hemisphere it is now the middle of winter. In the airport terminal, the atmosphere is a little oppressive with officials in uniforms that look like prison wardens who are placed in strategic positions and eyeing everyone with a hint of suspicion. I suppose it can only be expected as this is a political hotbed and not everyone's dream holiday because of the number of highly controversial unethical laws that are practised here.

The year is 1983 and the apartheid regime is still in full force. The white minority population have clung to power for many decades now, even though there is huge pressure for change from the rest of the world and also within the country itself, not just by the black majority, Indians and other non-white oppressed Africans but also by the minority white Democratic Party who have opposed the white ruling National Party on many issues of apartheid. Blacks still do not have the right to vote and are not represented in government.

Their movement is restricted, mostly to the rural areas in the vast country yet many live in designated areas set just outside the major cities. These are called 'Townships' where cheap housing is provided along with cheap transport to bus them into the city for work. By nightfall they are not allowed to be in the city unless they have a pass which is issued only to those working on night duty etc. These curfews and restriction on movement are a form of mass control which is the cause of so much protesting and international concern.

The National Party, however, maintains that because of the well-organised 'apartheid' system of white supremacy that South Africa is now the most prosperous and economically stable country on the whole African continent. They state that most of Africa is run by dictators where poverty, corruption and chaos are common. Work opportunities in South Africa are so much more abundant, that neighbouring workforce from countries like Mozambique, Zimbabwe, Zambia, Swaziland, Botswana and Lesotho are employed as migrant workers in the many gold and diamond mines, etc. This is all true but the argument is, that with these restrictions and without your basic freedom life becomes very oppressive and degrading.

So the reason I'm drawn here is uncertain and may only become clear once I've spent some time here, for I instinctively know that I will not always remain here as this is just a prominent station on my way. However, the sense of adventure that now opens the horizons of my mind is intriguing and I have a feeling of curiosity as I find my way out of the terminal building into the fresh morning air and the clear blue skies. I take a bus into the city centre of this sprawling metropolis and on the way we pass along the busy suburbs where there are groups of local blacks huddled together on the roadside around small makeshift fires to keep warm. It is still early morning and there is still a chill in the air even though the sun is out. I can feel the dry dust in the atmosphere and smell the burnt odour of the parched ground. It has a reddish hue that is common to most of Africa.

I am now beginning to sense the spirit of this vast continent that frees the shackles of the soul and brings a feeling of freedom and a joy of life. Maybe it is to do with the 'happy-go-lucky' attitude of the local people and the vast open spaces that still exist, where a variety of wild animals can roam free with gay abandon in many parts of the savannah. Just to see the annual great migration of the thousands of herbivores that cross the plains of the Serengeti and into the lush Masai Mara, brings a feeling of the awe that only nature can evoke.

When we arrived at the bus terminal/train station, it is strange to see only whites milling about in the complex. After all, this is Africa. But as I walk out into the streets and a couple of blocks up, I now see the segregation in full force as I come across another station terminal that is bustling with thousands of blacks jostling among the many hawkers selling their colourful wares. There are also many informal taxi's honking their horns and vying for passengers with music blaring in the mix of this chaotic scene. The atmosphere is overpowering to all the senses, yet I cannot pull myself away from the excitement. This is the real Africa with its intrigue that sucks you in, like a child at its first carnival fairground. There is a huge contrast of cultures that this division has caused but to be honest, it opens the mind with a feeling of wonder like you have just traversed from one continent to another in an instant.

After all the excitement, I head off towards the high-rise blocks of flats on the brow of the hill not far from the city centre. This is the suburb of 'Hillbrow', well known for its dense population of city workers made up of mostly European immigrants. No blacks are allowed to live in the inner-city areas, for their sprawling townships are located about five miles to the southwest of the of the city on the outskirts of this major industrial capital for reasons of so-called 'security'. Soon I arrive at a slightly run-down building marked 'Soper Lodge, Residential Hotel', where I have booked in for a few nights stay until I can find a 'bedsit' at a cheap rate, as I'm on a tight budget until I can get a half-decent job.

At the reception, there is no one around so I press the bell, and eventually, a tall gaunt white man about 30 sidles in and looks a little vague. When I explain that I have a reservation, he nonchalantly says in a heavy South African twang, 'Wait, someone will be out soon'. He must be another guest because he is strangely indifferent to my presence, and looks like he is on drugs or something. But I soon realise that this place is not what I expected and is a little eerie, so maybe I should be prepared to pay a little more for something better. As I sit waiting for a while, I get an uneasy feeling that I don't want to be here. So, I head for the door with my suitcase and escape into the street before anyone else has arrived. I feel a great sense of relief that I am now free to find something else in this very foreign city.

Eventually, I come across a YMCA which looks a lot more inviting, and there are many other immigrants new to the country who are staying here. I book into a dormitory which is even cheaper than the last place, and the atmosphere feels a bit more hospitable. When I wander outside into the now warm sunshine, I walk around the busy streets to acclimatise myself a little, and I begin to feel more at ease. Here, the blacks and whites mingle freely together, although each seem to be oblivious to the other as they weave along pavements and through the parks, quietly content and at ease.

Back in the dormitory that first night, the temperature plummets to around zero, and I can't sleep because of the biting cold. I had barely enough cover to suffice. I tossed and turned for what seemed like an age, and then just as I was about to fall asleep, there begins a few snorers, snoring in unison like a symphony. Then amid my frustration, I suddenly hear a clicking noise coming from the far end of the room. I slowly look around the dormitory of about 15 occupied beds, and then at the far end of the room, I spotted a young man with long blond hair, sat up in bed and clicking a flick knife repeatedly open and closed, with an angry frown on his face. I lay motionless for as long as I could in case he spotted me. Everyone else seems to be in La land. Eventually, I think I must have slept a little as the sun came shining through the curtainless windows to wake me.

I learnt later that the 'knife flicker' is an Afrikaner, who works in one of the many gold mines that are scattered in the sparse landscape that surrounds Johannesburg. Gold is the reason that this city sprung up in the first place less than a hundred years ago. The miners often come to seek out the 'bright lights' to get some relief from the harsh environment of a dreary regimented mining town and then splash their hard-earned 'bucks' in the bars, cafes, and clubs, with all kinds of entertainment in this hub that never sleeps. These miners are predominantly Afrikaans speaking yet they can speak English too as this is a dual lingual country. They actually form the majority of the whites in the whole of the country, although Johannesburg is predominantly English speaking. It's not the capital but it certainly is the biggest and it is the business centre. Pretoria is the nearby capital, which is mostly Afrikaans speaking and houses most of the government departments. In recent years, Johannesburg has become known more for its controversial politics rather than for its gold mines. It was here that Gandhi worked as a young lawyer, sent out by the Indian Government to represent the large Indian community and their many grievances with the apartheid system. After experiencing his own difficulties with the strict apartheid laws and being arrested, he soon set off back to India to take up the cause against white rule again. Then a few years later another 'freedom fighter' soon emerged here on the same dusty streets. Nelson Mandela came here after growing up and being educated in the rural southern parts of South Africa, to work in a legal firm and he worked his way up to be a lawyer, again representing the disadvantaged non-white population. It was here that he was arrested and found guilty of treason for attempting to bring down the government with planned attacks on the infrastructure, along with some other members from the now-ruling ANC organisation.

Over the next few days, I again walked, further in different directions to get a clear view of where I am staying and familiarise myself with my new city. Outside the inner city on the northern side, there are spacious wooded parks and wide tree-lined avenues with mansions along the way where the affluent whites live in luxury. These were originally built to house the mining magnates during the early rise of the gold rush.

Heading south and into the town centre, the streets are thriving with all chic boutiques, modern chain stores, and department stores that you can see in any large European city. In fact, apart from the multicoloured blend of cultures, it would be difficult to distinguish it from any city in the Western world. Johannesburg is less than one hundred years old, but it has risen at an alarming speed with many modern high-rise office blocks that rise up like a mirage on the flat plateau forming a modern oasis on the dry plains of the sparse highveld all around, which are occasionally broken up by gold mining dumps that are scattered nearby.

Close to the city centre is the suburb of Hillbrow where I'm located. It is crammed of high-rise residential flats that boasts one of the densest square miles in population along with Hong Kong.

I've been here a couple of days, and I'm now ready to start looking for a job as I only have enough money to last a few weeks. I have obtained a work permit already, which is easy enough as there is a demand for a foreign white workforce with much-needed skills. Later, when I get talking to another recent immigrant like myself, he asks me why I have chosen this city to settle and search for work, and not one of the more attractive coastal cities like Durban or Cape Town. I explain that it is here that most of the good job opportunities are. He then informs me that, "Johannesburg is known as the backside of Africa." Then he begins to tell me some stories about his experiences in the few months he's been here, and of course, he doesn't paint a pretty picture.

But I have lived in some of the rough northern cities in England before, so I am a little streetwise. However, I soon begin to realise that there is a dark and sinister feel about some parts of the city as there is in most large industrial cities. But this is a little more unnerving than I had first noticed. In Hillbrow where I am staying, there is a heavy feel of desperation in this crowded suburb, which along with the local white South Africans, there is a rich mixture of other cultures. Mostly, all are single men from different parts of Europe, searching for the promise of a new life with more opportunities, more money, more sunshine, and an outdoor lifestyle with lots of open spaces.

But many seemed to have hit the bottle out of loneliness and boredom, and the bars are filled with heavy drinkers as there is very little else to do here for entertainment in this concrete jungle and cultural desert. It resembles a modern version of the 'Wild West' with its recent history of the gold rush. There are many sanctions and a cultural boycott imposed on the whole country because of the apartheid regime with its attempts to keep the black majority in check. So it is quite difficult for most Europeans to settle, with little else to do but work, and they often end up drinking heavily in the seedy bars and clubs scattered in abundance in this high-rise flatland. Alcoholism is common here, and there are even quite a few foreign tramps who have bitten the dust and ended up sleeping in doorways and the few parks in the area.

I recognise the Scouse, Scottish, Welsh, Irish, and German accents, etc., as they try to converse with passers-by to beg a few coins for another drink. The lack of female energy has obviously contributed to the general mood of boredom. Overall, there is still an optimism in the air as many are seeking a new start to find a worthwhile career and perhaps a new lifestyle with some meaning or at least some outdoor adventure or purposeful direction. And I can vouch for that, for this is why I'm here, looking for that 'something', driven by a sense of adventure. Creativity is rarely born out of a life of ease and comfort. It is literally, sink or swim here as there is no social security or handouts for the displaced in society or the simply unemployed.

Hillbrow's flat land is then really only a stepping stone for new arrivals if they make it out of the rat race. There are also many of the younger South Africans who have sought some independence from family life, as rent prices are cheap here and jobs in the nearby business district are plentiful.

I begin applying for jobs and there are good opportunities if you are experienced. My previous work was in retail management; however, I was willing to find anything reasonable for now just to get started before I looked for a new career, which will take me out of retailing altogether. I need a new start in something a little more creative to suit my personality.

My skills at school were more artistic than anything else, so why I went into the business world of retailing I really don't know. Ideally, I would have liked to have gone to art school, but my parents were against that, as the recent hippy culture had killed that idea and my father would once again repeat those words which still ring in my ears even now, "Get a real job!" Because, having had an older cousin who had been to the local art school and now dressed and looked like Jesus Christ. He lived in a bedsit, unfurnished and yet he decorated it with public road signs he had illegally acquired. My father said he was not just 'unemployed' but 'unemployable'.

Alternatively, I would have liked to become a professional footballer, but that avenue of pleasure was also blocked by my father. Realistically, I was not built for the rigours of that sport as I was quite scrawny as a teenager. To be honest with myself, I lacked any ambition at the point of leaving school and just drifted into the easiest option available to me at the time. I was still quite immature. I considered myself as a late developer, but now that I was much older, I feel that I have broken free from the shackles of my limiting family upbringing and the futile existence that seemed to face me, and now maybe I am destined for something worthwhile.

Soon I get a job in a nearby hotel working in the bar. The hours are long into the night and the pay is not great, so that doesn't last long. Then back into retailing, working as an assistant in a hardware store. But I soon get the feeling I'm stagnating again. Even the manager had noticed that this was not going to last as he began calling me 'Nafi'. When I asked him what it meant, he explained 'No Ambition, Fuck'all Interest'. I stick this out for a few months as I try to fathom out what I can apply myself to and check out the options being offered.

Then one day I see an advert for a 'Silk-Screen Printing' supervisor. During my art 'A' level at school we did some silk-screen printing, so I had an idea what it entailed. I applied for the position, and my application is accepted for an interview in about ten days' time. Having had no working experience at this kind of job, I borrow a book from the library all about industrial silk-screen printing and read up about it. At the interview, I could see I was a bit out of my depths as the job involved heavy machinery and mass production of screen-printed drawing sheets for architects' studios. The interviewer must have had a sixth sense and seemed to see straight through me.

However, I must have been the only person to apply, because with a wry smile, the boss offered me the job knowing that I'd bullshitted my way through the interview. But I knew this was what I wanted, and it was going to give me the break that I needed for my creative urge, so maybe that's what came across in the meeting. Based on the colour of my skin, I was put in charge of the department, with three black workers and two semi-automatic printing machines. Silk-screen printing is an ancient Chinese form of printing that uses a process of squeezing ink or paint through a silk mesh that has had a desired design stencilled on to it.

It is popular with large format printing i.e. Highway posters and also materials that a normal Lithographic printing press cannot accommodate, like plastic or metal. Of course, these days pure silk fabric is no longer being used in this process, since much stronger made-made fabrics like polyester or nylon are more hard-wearing and more economical. I soon learnt all about the process and had the department running smoothly. After three years of perfecting the business, and now even married with two small children and a rented three-bedroomed house in the suburbs, I was becoming restless and needed something more challenging than just working 9 to 5 for a wage with no real foreseeable prospects. I wasn't the type to slowly wait in the wings until my turn came to climb the corporate ladder, so I took another leap forward.

Chapter 3
Breaking Free

I decided to branch out on my own to give me more freedom to become creative with new designs and have more control of my time. I opened a small factory with a simple and inexpensive hand-operated silk-screen machine called a 'carousel' that specialised in printing on cotton T-shirts and for clothing fabric in general. I had a premises along with two or three staff members, and now I had to search for clients in the rag trade with retail shops that could sell my printed designs.

I continued printing designs that were in fashion or even corporate clothing designs for companies with their own personal logos, for promotions and advertising. Having worked previously in the retail fashion for many years, I realised that it had now served a purpose for me to understanding the forever-changing trends and how the demands are marketed by the manufacturers and shops. Soon I was getting small orders here and there. I was well set up now and ready to look for bigger clients and bigger orders from the likes of wholesalers and chain stores.

But I was going to have to come up with new and original designs and the latest trends. With the country being sanctioned from virtually the whole global market, I began to take a look at the European shops while on my frequent visits home to see family and friends back in England. I visited some of the major cities to see what the designs were in the trendiest shops. Even when I had returned back to my factory back in South Africa, I managed to persuade my mother to scour the fashion shops and flea markets in the UK for new designs.

One particular incident was when I had seen a T-shirt print on a British comedy sitcom on South African TV. The T-shirt was called 'Captain Condom', which was a cartoon of Superman flying through the air with a condom on his head. So my mother, being in her middle sixties at the time, would never usually even frequent flea markets as she only shopped in places like Jaeger and Burberry's. She was now traipsing through Leeds and Wakefield outdoor flea markets in her pleated tweed skirts, asking every clothing stall if they had 'Captain Condom' T-shirts, much to the puzzlement of these casual traders.

One particular elderly stall holder's eyes lit up, and he must have thought his lucky day had arrived. She eventually found the design and posted it to me. With many new designs, I now had a head start as the European fashions took time to filter through to the far reaches of the globe. I soon got a huge order after I began to show the newly acquired designs around the high streets of Johannesburg. They were mostly ripped-off designs, it is true; however, I did try to modify them in some way because I felt a tinge of guilt about it and that I was not being creative enough.

Eventually, a well-known fashion group had placed an order of 15,000 T-shirts to be printed with a selection of my prints. I had only a few weeks to produce them. I bought another carousel printing machine and took on two more staff, then worked almost through all the nights that followed. Orders came in fast after that, and keeping up with demands now became my biggest challenge. What started off as printing T-shirts felt like I was printing money, and it seemed I had hit a niche in the market where everything just falls into place.

I was now divorced and living alone, and apart from monthly visits from my two children, I spent most of my time building the business. My lifestyle began to get so hectic as I was working flat out during the day and then, after hours, clubbing most nights just to cope with the stress building up. It was the only way I knew how to deal with the pressure. Things began to get out of hand when I got involved in some copy right infringements on famous brands that I was reproducing. The country had recently gone through a huge political change as the previous white minority regime began to collapse, and all citizens were eventually given the right to vote. Sanctions and boycotts were lifted, and now fashion labels that were once banned here were back and trading again. Before that, there were many manufacturers supplying fake copies that were being sold in the shops and with no repercussions. I was guilty of that temptation too.

The fraud squad got information about me from shops or flea market traders. They soon visited my premises and found goods that I had printed that were now contraband. They also found lots of political promotional prints that I had produced for the once-banned and exiled political organisations, like the predominantly Zulu, Inkatha Freedom Party and the well-known ANC Party, who eventually became the ruling party after a landslide election.

The white police force were still in charge of the country until the first free elections. So, finding me with thousands of T-shirts with opposition leader and the future President Mandela giving the 'black power' sign, etc., seemed to make them wonder who I really was and what I was up to, so they took me down to the police station for questioning. The heavy-set Afrikaans officer was named Kruger. He pulled up a chair in front of me and arranged himself in a conspiratorial position with a patronising smile that was very intimidating, as he grilled me about the goods in question.

I was allowed to light up a cigarette, aware of my senses now being ultra-sensitive as the acrid fumes stung my nostrils. I explained that I was only the printer producing for my client and besides I don't think they had a case against me as the situation in the country was about to change drastically. I was reprimanded about printing copyright goods then released after a few hours, with a good heart. They even asked me to become an informer, which I obliged, but after the first time, I stopped because it just didn't feel good. One of the cops even kept in touch and became a regular customer of mine, popping in to buy clothes for his family and friends at wholesale prices, of course.

I now refrained from printing contraband goods and concentrated on the designs that clients asked me to come up with. From then on, the business expanded steadily until I had to take on a partner to help with the pressure building up inside the factory and in my head. I took on a dynamic lady who was already familiar with the fashion trade in Johannesburg and with some good retail connections, as things really took off now. The orders and the money were rolling in faster than we could keep up. A friend of mine from my social life came to join us, working in the factory to help supervise the heavy workload.

His name was Peter. He was a borderline character who had a charming personality, albeit with a slightly dark side and somehow quite cleverly, operated just under the radar. Therefore, he always got away with things, knowing just when to lay low and when to move. He was a very passionate character and tended to do things in extremes with an over-indulgent nature.

That's when things really began to heat up because he was a small-time drug user, and he introduced my partner and me to amphetamines, which helped with the long hours and high demand, as it gave us that extra edge to cope. We seem to have hit on a magic formula because it felt like everybody wanted a piece of us. The film *Scarface* with Al Pacino and the power of cocaine use came to mind. We began to feel untouchable, and everything was moving so fast, and business was pouring in as we enjoyed the power of success and the money that was flowing our way.

Large fashion chains were seeking us out. People with shops as far as Durban, Cape Town, Botswana, and Swaziland would arrive at our premises and place orders. Word of mouth had spread so fast that we had to put off small-time traders who were too careful to commit to large orders, unless they paid cash up front, of course. We could not resist the power of cash and sometimes even sold our stock on-site that had been promised for large chain retailers, mostly because those larger chains insisted on 30 to 60-day terms of payment after delivery.

We had become ruthless and had few scruples now that we were in so much demand. 'Cash was king' for our newly required wealth that had caught us by surprise. Even the suppliers from the far east were arriving at our door, hoping to jump on the bandwagon and offering us containers of the latest fashions being produced in the now-booming economy of China since the decline of communism. We were the 'Talk of the Town', and there even appeared an article in a well-known magazine on the fashion trends taking South Africa by storm, in which we featured with a front-page photo of a range of our clothes.

Life was good while it lasted, with fast cars and trips to the faraway places. However, inevitably, it eventually got out of hand as life in the factory started to go chaotic with the three of us trying to keep control while being high on speed, and more and more orders coming in. It was a recipe for disaster, and the more chaotic it got, the more 'speed' we took, and the bigger our egos got. Apart from the mounting tension, there was the loss of weight and slight signs of ill health that we were all beginning to experience, which eventually led to paranoia. Paranoia is the beginning of the end because that's when doubt sets in and trust is lost, and everything we took for granted as just fate was now affecting our inflated egos which soon began to crack.

We began to lose control of the finances and accounts, each suspecting the other of creaming money from the business, and so we became progressively distant towards each other through suspicion and mistrust. Our 15 members of staff were hopefully all oblivious to what the real issues were. This went on for some time while we tried to get through the workload. But something had to give as it was getting ever increasingly toxic in the factory. First, we had to get rid of my friend Peter who by now was barely functional and starting to affect the staff who were now also becoming paranoid by all the negative energy swirling around.

Then I had 'burn out' soon after discovering that I was indeed being scammed by my partner and I could not even face coming into work at all because of the heavy atmosphere and my disturbed mental state, so I said I wanted out and I quit. My partner could have the business for all I cared, and she paid me a small fee to walk away, which I was glad to accept even though I had lost the very business I had started. My desire and drive were no longer in it. The fun had gone from the desire to create my own piece of the world, and maybe it would have lasted if I had stayed honest and been content to keep to my own talents even if it meant staying small and developing much slower.

Yet I felt I had reached a top dog status in this chosen path with all the money and recognition, even though it was hollow achievement. One of the greatest drives in nature is to satisfy our animalistic desire to dominate and be seen to succeed for then we have greater choice and so-called freedom, let alone the ego's need for recognition and approval. However, I was hugely disillusioned by all the success and money.

I felt deluded with a false sense of freedom and my ego had now been deflated! I needed a break just to get my sanity back and see where I was at before deciding what I was going to do next. The burnout I suffered led me into a deep depression which I would go in and out of for the next few years!

Chapter 4
The Seeker

The next few months were tricky. Trying to come down from those highs was tough, and I had moments of extreme peace mixed with anxiety pangs. I had lost the easy-going attitude I once had before I first got started in all this. I had become the kind of man I had always hated. These words are from a song in the 1990s, *Born of Frustration* by the band James.

I remember my best friend and I promising ourselves when we had reached twenty that we would try to remain the same 'young hearts' all our lives, but now at forty, I felt like a 'stuffy old sod'. Over the previous eight years or so, I had been drinking and womanising heavily since my divorce. I messed around every weekend just to fill the emptiness that was inside me. Most of the women were one-night stands, and some I didn't even know their names.

After a few drinks, I didn't care who it was or what they looked like. I slept with Black women, Coloured, White, Chinese, Indian, fat, anorexic, plain, and the pretty ones too. I then got bored with the small talk that was required to charm someone into bed, so I began frequenting striptease joints and drinking places where prostitutes would hang out. They were usually cheap joints where there was an abundance of women from all walks of life and all parts of Africa and some beyond.

The prices were cheap, and if they liked you a lot, they would let you stay the night and wouldn't even charge. One of the seedy clubs I frequented was called the 'Pink Pony'. It was a plush place that used to be a smart hotel in its hey-day. It was fairly large, very busy, and well-run by a prominent Greek businessman who owned it. The law must have eventually turned a blind eye because they used to raid the place often, but now, as time went by, I used to see a police car parked outside, and they seemed more interested in keeping the peace than shutting the place down.

Rumour had it that they were paid protection money. It was not exactly 'the place to be seen', but it was there that I encountered some surprise secret visitors who were from the rag trade, and I remember thinking that they were the last people I would expect to see here. My first thought was, "What's a nice guy like you doing in a dump like this?" But they could well have thought the same thing of me. Because it was my secret double life too!

However, one particular place I visited was a large country house just outside Johannesburg called 'The Ranch'. It was very high class, and the women were expensive. Entrance was by membership only or invitation from a member. I knew some Taiwanese fashion traders who frequented it, and so I got in when I was feeling like splashing out. The hostess was a pantomime dame with her large, satin-clad bosom, lacquered set hair, and a shingled neck. She knew how to entertain and had some of the most beautiful-looking women I had ever encountered.

It all felt good at first because I felt it was filling the emptiness in me. I thought I was healing, but eventually it eats you up, and then you begin to feel nothing inside—not pleasure, not joy, and no sense of fun. The lack of emotions of this kind of encounter is soul-destroying. The intimacy in the beginning gradually fades, and it doesn't mean much anymore. It must be like working as a surgeon where cutting people open becomes unemotional and detached.

It's just a lump of flesh, but at least they are working for a good cause. For me, it was all about me! Most of these kinds of women could say they are doing it for a reason because usually, their need is money and therefore survival. One of the prostitutes I had known was on the game to support a baby; eventually, she committed suicide, leaving the baby to be supported by the state. It destroys both souls.

A psychologist I saw a few months later explained to me that, "When men get divorced from a destructive marriage they often set about to get revenge on all women, by sleeping around, fucking them, and leaving them!" I think that was a bit harsh, for deep down I was looking for affection. However, I was rarely emotionally attached to any of them, and if there was a glimmer of love, it never lasted long before I was on to my next conquest. I was slowly self-destructing, like a slow suicide, much like an alcoholic or drug addict does.

My drug was sex! This was my addiction that I was only to realise much later. It's not pretty, but it feels like some movement in the right or wrong direction; it doesn't matter which because stagnation is worse. I had begun to feel some regret as the emptiness inside eventually grew bigger. The hopelessness and the loneliness of my sordid existence was complete. Depression was the result of the years of my refusal to see my downward spiral and to ignore all the warnings as I was self-destructing.

I had been doing all this while trying to maintain a good business-like image to all the people I dealt with and help raise two children in school, but now I was living a double life and it was leading me towards rock bottom. I was sinking into solitude and began to distance myself from everyone, even from the seedy clubs and the womanising too. I stayed home or went for lonely walks in the wild. I was now suffering withdrawal symptoms, losing weight and sinking into deeper depressions. I was out of self-esteem and void of emotion. I didn't know it then but all this had been an attempt to get something out of my system. I was no longer tempted by this 'forbidden fruit', although the urge was still there, like a smoker's craving for nicotine! Hitting rock bottom is the surest way to change because from here on the only way is up. I had now also given up smoking and drinking as well as amphetamines. But of course, this void I created would eventually need to be filled! I would need to find a way back to myself.

I felt like the Tin Man in *The Yellow Brick Road*, who was empty inside with no soul. The mornings were the worst. I would wake, wandering how I was going to get through another long day. I would wake in my dreary flat, implicated by every banal object. Its black curtains, black furniture, and the pointless junk all around. My shoes both lying there in the middle of the carpet, one hopelessly on its side. Even brushing my teeth was a painful effort to get my day started.

Just going to the local shop to get groceries was hard because it meant I had to face up to someone. I needed to find my centre, but misery begets more misery and makes life a spiral ever heading down. I had dug myself into a deep hole that I found I couldn't seem get out of!

I had to reinvent myself quickly because I had to start working again soon as I still had two children to feed, a mortgage, and expenses to keep up. But the undoing of 20 or more years of my cultural ideals and draconian beliefs was not going to be easy. Christ said, "you have to empty the old wine before you can taste the new wine." So I set about to break down the rigid mindset and negative judgements that had held me down for so long.

Going to motivational talks and seminars, I was inspired for a while but this kind of motivation only lasts as long as a hot meal. I needed something more. I was in need of a complete overhaul because burnout leaves you with a feeling that something is constantly missing, like an engine firing on only three cylinders. I was alive but I was not living because there was something in my psyche that felt unbalanced.

This uneasy feeling gnaws away at you like a dull toothache, sapping all your energy in an attempt to force you to confront yourself, pushing you further to the edge of chaos. To a point where you either retreat back to ways of old or move further into chaos. I just wanted to be free. Freedom from this oblivion!

So I delved further into my misery and began cutting myself off from my past life and the few friends I still had until I reached a deeper desperation and loneliness. It was at this point that I knew I needed help!

In the meantime, I started up on my own again in the clothing business, but this time I knew that anything as labour-intensive as before was the last thing I needed. I wanted to stay in the clothing business as I had many contacts, and it was basically all that I knew. I was going to take things easy from now and try to remember to stay present and enjoy the process without getting carried away by the goals. It is an old cliché, I know, but I was grateful that I now had a second chance to find success without it going to my head.

Now I had to try to feel some sense of achievement and job satisfaction and, of course, without the substance abuse. I decided to open a clothing warehouse where I would only buy and then supply clothing to the fashion houses, mostly imported goods from the far east as about 90% of all clothing was coming from countries like China and Taiwan now that world sanctions were lifted since the end of the old apartheid regime. Communism had also changed and made some U-turns so I travelled to China to visit some of the factories and showrooms.

I personally knew some Chinese importers and I began ordering goods and stocked up with the latest styles. I opened a showroom too, so that clients could come in and browse the goods in stock and buy on the spot. For larger orders, I would import from my Chinese connections and have them shipped in. It started off well and carried on growing over the next couple of years.

But my psyche was still disturbed as the depression kept coming back in spells now. Something in my life was still amiss. I had managed to rid myself of the drug habit and had stopped drinking and partying, but that just left a huge void. I decided to go and see a psychologist but that was hopeless too, as the psychologist seemed more lost than I was and then prescribed me some drugs, but they didn't help either. Besides, that was the last thing I needed, for it was likely that drugs got me into this mess in the first place. It wasn't a shrink that I needed more like an 'Exorcist'! I needed something more proactive and much deeper than just medication to nullify me. I needed to get to the root cause to rescue myself from this dilemma.

H G Wells wrote, "Just remember, if you don't like your life you can change it." The answer is that simple. But in reality, the process of changing the whole of your life's thinking takes a tremendous effort of continued discipline because we are creatures of habit and it can take years to break just one habit. The first thing I would have to do was to build up some mental strength and discipline myself because I felt that I had become weak-willed and lost, with no real direction in my life. My mind was scattered from all the hectic self-indulgent years of living a life of a 'libertine', doing whatever I wanted, whenever without any consideration of the consequences. My lifestyle of drink and womanising had taken control of me.

There is an old Chinese proverb that says, "A man had a drink, the drink had a drink, the drink had the man."

I had realised that, 'Freedom is not doing what you want'! I began to see that if it was freedom that I was looking for then I would have to have some control of my mind and begin to learn how to direct my thoughts towards some particular goal instead of just living a life without much thought in my head, drifting towards a futile existence. I began meditation and I soon observed that my mind was indeed flitting from one place to the next with no control of thought!

Chapter 5
Out of Body

That's was when I had a strange experience. I had been sitting in a restaurant lounge having a quiet drink with my old friend Steve, whom I had called up to try and share what I was now going through in an attempt to solve my dilemma with the way I'd been feeling recently. I was quite relaxed after a stressful week at work. We were both sitting on the same sofa having a sundowner when I suddenly left my physical body and began to float up to the ceiling. From there I was looking down on my body that was next to my friend Steve.

I just hung up there for a while, and the feeling was wonderful, like being in another world, yet I was fully awake and aware of the room around me and all the other guests mingling. The place I went to felt so real that it made living in the here and now dreamlike in comparison. After only a few seconds, I came back into my body reluctantly and was amazed by what had just happened right there in a crowded place, yet I knew that not even Steve was aware of it, so I remained quiet and somewhat stunned by this 'out of body experience'. I ordered another coffee although I really didn't want one because I was unlikely to get much sleep that night anyway.

This incredible moment went against all I ever believed in. I was very materialistic and thought that what you see in this physical world is all there is. I was not religious or spiritual in any way yet here there was; some 'other' invisible entity or being that was a part of me that had the ability to rise up, move out of my body and it could even see with invisible eyes. It shook the very foundation of my belief system, not that I had much of one, other than scepticism.

I couldn't shake off this feeling of deja vu, that I had already lived through this scene. As a young child when I was sick in bed with fever, I seemed to remember being awake in another world. It was a beautiful feeling but I just shrugged it off eventually, not knowing what it could be, at such a young age. I never even mentioned it to my mother at the time.

I began questioning everything I thought I knew and even started to become open to the 'absurd'. Things like ghosts, poltergeists, and entities from other realms. My normal three-dimensional world was now thrown into doubt. The foundation of our individual personality is based on what we know and what we believe to be true without much doubt. But now this one event had turned my whole world upside down. It caused a shift in my psyche that changed my normal state of awareness.

My confidence was now becoming shaky. It began to affect my business because now I was not so sure that I was even in control of that or much of my life at all. I had usually been so cocksure of myself and that whatever I put my mind to, I had usually succeeded in most cases. I thought I had been directing my life so far up until this point because I had the power to take control of events and make things happen for me to some extent. I considered myself a fairly successful member of the community around me, with my own thriving business, my house, and a pretty hectic social life and a family with children, even though it was a broken family because of divorce.

But now I realised that within me there was a higher power that seemed to be overseeing all my events. I now began to question everything before I accepted it into my new ideals of my now fragile life. I started to become pensive and a little withdrawn as I continually reflected on what it was that I had seen on that fateful day. The worst thing about all of it was that there was no one that I could confide in because virtually everyone I knew would have thought I was losing the plot. Anyway, it was impossible for me to adequately describe what I saw and felt! Mary C. Neal in her book called *To Heaven and Back* tries to describe her near-death experience. "I feel as though I am trying to describe a four-dimensional experience while living in a three-dimensional world. The appropriate words, descriptions, and concepts don't exist in our current language and it is the cause of much limitation."

The only person who might at least listen to what I had to say was possibly my mother, but when I told her even she thought I was losing it and appeared concerned for my sanity. Sometime later, when I told her that I was attending a Sikh temple on weekends, she was convinced I had been recruited by some crazy 'cult'. I was now completely on my own.

The most profound experience in my life and I had to keep it to myself just to avoid ridicule because no one was taking me seriously. Most people just thought it was some kind of delusional moment of delirium and that I must have been imagining things. So, I withdrew more and more into my thoughts and yet I had to maintain as much normality as I could in business and with friends and family.

That is when I met an old Chinese man called Mr Lee, on a plane coming back from Hong Kong after a buying trip to China. We had been seated next to each other by some coincidence or by fate? He had been on this trip to source any traders who might be interested in importing T-shirt fabric that had been already sized and cut ready to be assembled in a factory in South Africa.

This process was unusual, but it meant that any import duty was avoided as the goods were not complete and therefore were destined for a final process of assembly in a South African factory. Much like the car industry operates here, being put together at an assembly plant to avoid import duty.

Mr Lee was a wise old man who appeared calm and at peace with himself, and we chatted about various subjects on the state of the psyche of modern man and the difference between the Western world and Eastern philosophy. He had such a vast knowledge of the occult mysteries of life and of different beliefs and religions. I even questioned why he was even involved in simply trading of fabrics. His reply was that "his goal in life was to become invisible," moving between the higher worlds and the world of physical reality, much like a leopard moves through the bush undetected.

It was like he was an 'Undercover Messiah'! In this way, by going about his life as any normal person, he could hopefully be recognised by genuine seekers of the truth, because there was an air about him that intrigued and drew in anybody with a hint of curiosity. He said, "the more genuine you become, the more mysterious you appear" and that "not all enlightened beings become spiritual leaders but that some can even be found working on a supermarket checkout, just being a 'light in the community'."

He explained, "that most of us like to believe we are independent and in control but in reality we are virtually all living a life of the 'herd mentality' and true individuality is rare as it means breaking out of the confines and sways of the ego and rising up on a path of self-discovery to live in the state of the 'Higher Self' as it is known."

I had read a passage in the book *Desert Rose* written by Chinese writer Mary Weijun Collins about life in communist China under Mao Tse Tung. She says, "For the first time in my life, I realised no one was free in an interfering and conformist society, that the 'collective spirit' was the dominating principle and everybody had to do what society expected you to do. Individuality was not accepted, and you would be punished by the masses if you did something unacceptable to the social conventions. Mao and Communism had taken China back to the dark ages in his relentless quest to hold onto power. Even the Western world that I was bought up in, it is somewhat restricting but just more subtle!"

Mr Lee went on with a little story he had heard recently. "There was a man catching lobsters off the rocky coast near Cape Town. He had caught quite a few and had them in an open basket. A passerby asked him why the lobsters don't escape and just crawl out of the basket, back into the sea. The fisherman replied, 'Because they are South African lobsters and they will keep clinging on to each other, pulling each other back'!"

I realised it was incredible to see how wrapped up we are in other people's lives and how we react because of the way we think others would like us to. Mr Lee went on, "Our quest then is the 'path of honesty'. 'Being true to thyself' as the ancient Greeks coined it." He explained, "that when one sets out to seek the 'truth' and rises up to higher states of consciousness, then this process automatically opens up the dark side of the ego which causes a disturbance that most people are not prepared to confront because it threatens to shatter the fragile ego that we have been protecting most of our lives by building multiple personalities to avoid annihilation."

The Latin word 'persona' means mask, and we build different masks for the ego to hide behind in different circumstances. The path of honesty exposes our unconscious fears and secrets, revealing the authentic character behind the ego," he went on. "If only the seeker can listen to their heart and trust the process because you cannot find God with mere intellect. It requires the power to dream. Let go and just sink down beneath your conscious 'like a stone beneath the water' to your rightful level in the world in which you find yourselves, right here in the now! This process can take months, years, or a lifetime. Each soul's journey has a unique path, and with it, the right time will come to pass."

Soon, I began attending a Tibetan Buddhist meditation group where we were firstly told to sit still and try to feel if there was any tension in our body. I could feel that my tension was in my jaw as I seemed to be gritting my teeth constantly. After many sessions just learning to sit still and let go of all the tension in my body, I began to see where I needed to get. The next lesson was to be aware of my thoughts, and I realised that in fact, my mind was like a butterfly flitting from one place to the next and that I had very little concentration in any one direction. I soon learnt how to be in more control of my thoughts instead of my thoughts being in control of me. This, I was told, was what the Buddhists call 'Mindfulness' and it became a daily practise from then on because the mind is likened to a muscle and the more you exercise, the stronger it gets.

However, this exercising requires a regular daily practice of letting go of the mental activity and then trying to hold the mind still. The mind can be incredibly powerful and acts like a magnifying glass, which, when held still, and only then like the magnifying glass, does it become more powerful. Professional athletes understand this concept when focusing on one point to get the best concentration needed. The power of belief is also extremely important when applied to the mind because whatever is continually fed into the mind through thoughts, either good or bad, will eventually manifest! Thoughts and dreams are much like seeds being planted into the mind which eventually, with some cultivation and nurturing, will emerge into a reality, like a miracle. Whatever you put out into the universe is what will come back to you. If you want to become a millionaire or an artist, then by indulging in thoughts of becoming one and believing it to be true is the surest way to get there, eventually.

If you want something enough, all the universe conspires in helping you achieve it. I realised all these ideas were not exactly new concepts. Christ said to his disciples when they asked at the last supper, "How should we pray?" He replied, "Believing you have received it, ye shall receive it." Miracles, therefore, can be performed by anyone, any time, whether they are religious or not. The mind is that powerful.

For the next few months, I wandered around many days like a lonely cloud, never finding any lasting peace because I could not find any purpose. I could not go back to living with the same old life I once had anymore. I had just been going through the motions of living. I was alive, but was I really 'living'? Shortly after this experience, I had an insight come to me in the evening just before sleep. It felt as though some one was talking to me, yet I heard no voice but just the words that came to my mind. They were the name of a book, *Out on a Limb*, by Shirley MacLaine. It was a book I had heard about because I was a great admirer of this beautiful actress from my past, being a lovestruck teenager. But I had little idea what it was about, so I managed to get the book a few days later.

The theme was that 'nothing in the universe happens by accident' and it's basically about many phenomenal events that were going on in her life at the time, including her experiences 'Out of body'. She had even made a film, *Out on a Limb*, about her experiences. I began reading other books about Astral travel, near-death experiences, many of the well-known poets, and any subject that related to the mysteries of the unknown world. I bought Dr Scott Peck's *The Road Less Travelled*. I read *The Third Eye* by Lobsang Rampa. Fascinated by the subject, I delved into it as much as I could. I joined the Sikh temple for a while. I went to see an African Sangoma, visited a Jewish synagogue, a mosque, and I even joined a spiritual circle listening to 'Mediums' channelling. I visited many different religious services just to see if there were any similarities. I did ten-day fasts, drinking only liquids. I walked for hours in the African bush, hoping for a sign. I read ancient scriptures, hoping to decode them. I learnt dream interpretation. I did charity work and sometimes gave money. I was trying everything to see if it had any effect on my mind.

I did have some occasional peak experiences which were more like a feel-good factor, so I kept on. The answers I was looking for seemed to be in the 'mysteries' of the uncharted psyche. I was attempting to delve into the depths of the subconscious, that little-known part of the mind that many have attempted to understand. I read stories like, Conrad Hilton's, who had started the Hilton hotel group. How he bought his first property site to build an international hotel on, from a closed auction. The potential buyers were asked to submit their highest price in a sealed envelope. The night before all the submissions were due, Conrad had a dream that he had put 40,000 dollars on his submission. So the following day, he did just that, and his was the highest bid by a very short margin, and the property was his. Another example of the subconscious in dreams was the inventor of the common sewing machine. Mr Elias Howe had been trying for years to build this machine, but he could not figure out how it was going to work and was about to give up in frustration when he had this dream. He saw a tribe of savages who had thrown him into a stewing pot. They had spears that looked just like large sewing needles. Only the difference was that the eye of the needle was at the pointed end. That's when he realised the eye in the needle in his machine should be at the other end and 'voila', that's how the sewing machine was invented!

The subconscious is not just accessed through dreams but can come as ideas, intuition, and insights in moments of inspiration. 'Joan of Arc' heard voices from God, yet they must have been 'Ideas of inspiration', because when she was questioned at her trail for heresy before being burnt at the stake, the judge asked her, "What language God spoke to her in?" She replied, "I don't know what language he spoke, but I heard them in French." This is often how many poets, writers, inventors, business people, and artists create their ideas. These ideas mostly come when we least expect them. Sometimes the more we try to think about something, the further away it appears. When we let go of the struggles of the mind and logical thinking, that's often when answers come in with ease.

Mr Lee had quoted a Zen saying, "No thinking no mind, No mind no problem." Of course, this is often contradictory to the Western thought of 'Mind over matter'. All this mystical stuff was not just ideas to me but had some significance because all the time I felt like I was being induced to go further and further like I was on a magical mystery tour and along the way there were little treasures being revealed. Although, how to bring on a mystical experience of phenomenology was still a puzzle but as the years went by, I could say I felt lighter and saw some direction to my once wayward life. Yet paradoxically, there were very dark days and long periods of no movement when I wandered around in much confusion and which felt like I was in a cul-de-sac. It was like I had lost the connection and wasn't sure if it would ever come back again! However, after bumping into Mr Lee at one of these times, he had explained, "that this was a common experience, often called the 'dark night of the soul' and was a sure sign that you are truly 'on the path'. In fact, it is moments like this that much progress is actually made after breaking through the struggle, and it is usually only in hindsight that the past can be appreciated."

Chapter 6
Initiation into Another Reality

That's when I heard about the 'Awakening'. There was an advert on the local radio, headed 'Entering the World of Other Realities'. They were inviting participants to spend a 6-day retreat in a private lodge on a game reserve. It was two Canadians, Ben and Rob, who had been initiated into the Canadian Indians shamanistic practice of healing, vision quests and entering other realms in our mystical universe. They maintained that through a series of rituals and practices on a sacred workshop that our subconscious minds could be accessed more freely resulting in mystical experiences. There's nothing much new about this as there are plenty of religious sects promising a quick trip to heaven, but this seemed different because it was not being offered in the name of religion and had no ties attached. Yes, there was a fee to pay that was not cheap, but I would rather pay for a good service than get a freebie that has little energy. Besides, money does create its own energy.

I went for an interview and was asked about my religious beliefs and reasons for showing interest in this programme. Having an open mind seemed to be the main requirement and there were some other minor details required but no promises or guarantees were made. In short, entering the unknown offered no definite outcome and there were no certificates. Each person was likely to have a different experience or at least react differently. Entering this unknown event without much information and at quite a price was a bit risky, but through my intuition, I personally had a good feeling about it and so took the plunge.

A few days later, I received an invitation to attend the workshop which was to be held in a few of months' time at a private game reserve lodge deep into the African bush somewhere. The entire lodge had been booked out for the 6 days, even the kitchen staff, etc., were brought in after being hand-picked, so there was maximum privacy. All participants were obliged to refrain from revealing what went on during the week-long 'Awakening course'. Not because they were trying to be secretive but because it may spoil it for anyone who had not been on this mysterious journey yet.

So now I am going to have to spare you the details of the course because I feel obliged to. But I felt I could reveal the effects it had on me and how it changed my circumstances. Before it started, we all had instructions sent on how to prepare for the initiation with a few things we were asked to do, like a daily walk just to make sure we were physically in a good space. And some emotional clearing of the psyche too, like letting go of any resentments towards people or past events, etc., also doing something beneficial for the community i.e. volunteering. Then just helping someone in need who was old or sickly or just doing something for someone without any reward. Like knocking on a stranger's door and handing them a bunch of flowers but claiming that you were only the delivery guy. This I did for a nearby neighbour and the reaction was wonderful. Also picking out someone you worked with who was normally not easy to get on with and telling them just how much you appreciated working with them, which was something I hadn't thought much about before. We also had to do some contemplating and affirmations in meditation, focusing on a powerful and a rewarding outcome for the upcoming course of events.

On the day of the departure, I had to travel an hour or so to the bush lodge where all the other rather apprehensive participants were assembled. The unknown adventure always has a mixture of feelings from anxious fear to excited anticipation, and this was the cause of the eerie silence that had descended on our group as we mulled around the reception area waiting for our first instructions. When we were arriving, the early mist was clearing, and we could hear the sounds of the bush. It was a sparse open area with acacia trees and soft dry sand. We were completely secluded from the outside world as a sacred place was essential for the initiation.

We were shown to our log cabins and given a short time to unwind before being called to a meeting to explain what the basic programme for the week ahead was going to be and some of the rules required of us. There were no radios, TVs, or newspapers allowed, and we had to hand in cell phones and watches. No alcohol or any other mind-altering substances. However, smoking was allowed in open areas. Each one of us was unknown to any other participant, and during the course, we were not allowed to talk about the future or the past to anyone else. Only the present. This is even more difficult than it sounds, but it meant that the whole time we were there we could not know who the others really were in their everyday life, i.e., what their jobs were, what their family circumstances were, where they were from, or their past history at all. It makes small talk almost impossible during any uncomfortable silences. But it was supposed to help keep us in the present, and it was certainly very difficult to begin with, but with practice, it became more natural and spontaneous, not knowing whether you were talking to an airline pilot or a street cleaner, a millionaire or a pauper. We were not even told the names of the other 30 or so participants, and so we were given new names that were popular names of wild animals that were common in these parts of the world. My name was Leopard; others were Lion, Zebra, Eagle, Turtle, and so on. All in all, it brought about greater authenticity from each one of us as we struggled to be in the moment with the raw vulnerability we were now thrown into.

We heard stories of the ancient mystics like Lao Tzu, Buddha, Christ, Krishna, and Sitting Bear, who have left their mark on society with their profound wisdom, and even some of the most recent ones, great men and women, sages and saints who have lived in our time and indeed some are still alive today. It's strange how we presume greatness only exists in the distant past when there are great men and women, geniuses with great wisdom and understanding, still alive today. We just don't make legends out of people any more until they are believed to be from the 'other worldly' past. And maybe that is rightly so, because Buddha said, "when I point to the moon, don't look at my finger." As the course progressed through the days, there was a constant feeling that we were entering altered states of mind, and life was becoming surreal. I was beginning to dream a lot at night, and sometimes my awakened state was becoming fuzzy and not so sure. Because of this unknown state of mind, I felt a lot of fear arising and felt extremely vulnerable. I was in the uncomfortable situation of being confronted by my innermost feelings of insecurity, like a festering wound was being opened up. With all these people around, it was like finding yourself dreaming that you are at work and naked. My once closed and secretly guarded emotions were now being revealed, and my ego was shattering around me, to the point I felt I was losing control of my mind, and the more effort I made to be in control, the more things were collapsing around me. I felt like all this emotional stuff was only happening to me, but then I realised each person was going through something of their own stuff. Some encouragement to keep going was offered with motivational stories, e.g., "A young monk who had been in a monastery for a couple of years began to be discouraged." So he approached the elder monk and asked in frustration, "How do you reach enlightenment?" So, the older monk took the young monk down to the river and asked him to get into the water. The young monk stepped in. At that point, the older monk took him by the head, submerged him under water, and held him down. At first, the young monk did not resist, but after a few seconds, the young monk, realising the elder monk was not letting go, began to struggle to free himself for air. But the elder monk persisted until the younger monk eventually using all his strength, managed to force himself free. At which point the elder monk said, "That's how you reach enlightenment. You have to want it like your next breath!"

Most of my encouragement came through my fellow participants, who I saw were crumbling, and yet time and time again, they would rally round each other in support or sometimes just go off alone into the wild for a while and then come back with renewed spirit. By the time the week was nearing an end, I felt I wasn't even sure what was real and what was not. My physical reality and dreams had become one. At some point, I even felt I had no mind. I couldn't even think.

A thought would form and then evaporate before I could follow it. I couldn't quite get a grasp of my mind. I sometimes felt dizzy, as if I was high up on the edge of a building without anything to grab hold of, as if I were going into an empty space, into an abyss. At another time, someone behind me put a hand on my shoulder, and I felt like I had been touched for the very first time as their energy surged right through me. When I turned round to see who this could possibly be, I realised it was one of the other participants.

We were all now connecting with each other and also with our own emotions on a deeper level. Giraffe was having a tough time, and I could see that she was on the brink of giving up, and it certainly made me think about following her if she decided to walk. That's when I recalled a scene from a favourite film I had seen many times. It is called *The Count of Monte Christo*.

There was a young man who had been locked up on a penal island in the Mediterranean with a life sentence for a crime he didn't commit. However, he had been in solitary confinement for a few years when all of a sudden, a fellow prisoner attempting to escape had tunnelled into his cell by mistake, for he had got his bearings wrong. He was a wise old man, played by Richard Harris, and the young prisoner was intrigued by the old man's calm presence and mature wisdom. Together they agreed to start another tunnel out and seek to escape. The old man said it had taken him seven years to tunnel so far and that it would probably take another seven years to tunnel out. The young man replied in frustration, "I can't wait that long." To which the wise old man calmly replied, "Have you got anything better to do?"

So I stuck it out and struggled on. However, it was the next piece of advice that changed everything for me, when Rob said, "Whatever you don't confront in this life's journey, then your children or their children will have to confront it." I knew then, once again, I had finally reached the 'point of no return'. This time it was psychological. I would now move forward and take responsibility for my life and the consequences of my actions.

I knew it was through the humiliation of my closely guarded ego that would open the doors to a new beginning by letting go of the past and facing up to whatever the future had in store. Alan Watts, the late philosopher said, "The self always escapes introspection," presumably because the ego always protects itself from annihilation. That's what I felt was happening to me. I was confronting the dark side of my ego and the barriers I had been hiding behind.

During one session on the penultimate day, when the tension was now so intense, I lay down to relax on the floor while we were all taking some time out from another long day. Suddenly, I felt something stir within my abdomen, and my chest area expanded. Could this be the physical part of the process of enlightenment? I felt I had broken through some invisible barrier that now left the future wide open. A new beginning lay in front of me like a vast open expanse. I now felt liberated from my closely guarded inhibitions. I had the scope of a 'bird's eye view' as opposed to my normal worm's eye view of the world around me.

Eventually, the last day arrived, and we all gathered to say goodbye to each other and the two leaders. Ben then said to me, "Have you got what you wanted?" It was only then that I realised that an 'Awakening' can only come through two enlightened masters, so there is no doubt or any chance of the initiate being deluded.

As I said goodbye to them, hoping that there was some 'back up' to entering this new world, I asked if we would be meeting up again in the future, but Ben just casually replied, "if our paths happen to cross again." So this is it! The journey of the rest of my life begins today, and it looks like it is going to be a path of solitude, for I just realised that no one can take the journey with you.

Had I gone too far, too high, too soon? I was now standing alone! There was something odd and nameless happening inside me. It had no shape but was as real as stone. I was living a different version of me, and it felt like the real me was watching from the outside without judgement as events casually passed.

I was beside myself This was my secret. Why tell?.

Chapter 7
New Wine

As I tried to come to terms with the changes in my life, they now started to feel more like a curse rather than a gift. I had been expected to live life in peace and harmony from now on, but this was not the case here. I struggled to get back to my normal routine of work, family, and even leisure. I felt like I had just fallen from paradise and was now living in the dungeon of the harsh world where the mundane had now appeared more mundane.

I had now found myself once again back in the world of normal everyday life. I could not maintain the power to see through this dense physical world confronting me even though I knew it was not all there was to reality. This natural world was more like a parallel image and the visual copy of paradise, but it was dependant on perception. Every now and then, that veil was drawn back, and the beauty of this 'other worldly' creation presented itself in all its glory, only to slowly cloud over those crystal-clear glasses, darkly again.

Then one day, an old Jewish man called Mr Segal walked into my warehouse to buy some samples of the clothing that I had in stock, which was quite an ordinary request, yet there was something about him that intrigued me. He was a large man with a thick beard and a calm aura about him. He seemed to have a knowing smile on his face, like he knew me from somewhere before. As we chatted a little more about life, he suddenly asked how my children were. To which I said, "They're okay." The way he asked me was as if he knew them personally, but I knew he couldn't have, and that it was just the manner in which he spoke.

After he left, I realised that on some deeper level, he could see through me or he had some knowledge about me. The next time he came in, he came with two toys and said they were for my children. Normally, if a stranger gave me a gift, I would wonder if there was some ulterior motive behind the gesture, but he was a likeable character, and I accepted them with gratitude. We chatted some more about life and the twists and turns that it takes unexpectedly, and he told me a little about what he was buying the clothing for. I had told him a little about the factory I was recently running that had caused my downfall and breakdown. He explained that it was probably the wisest move I had made to get out of manufacturing and concentrate on selling.

He explained that Jewish people rarely get involved in manufacturing as it is far too labour-intensive and restricting. With sales, there is no limit to the amount of goods you can sell, and so it makes more sense to let others do the hard work of production. Besides, the hardest workers in life are usually always the least paid. However, it was only later that I learnt from another Jewish customer of mine who told me about Mr Segal's past. He had a large company that went bust, and he lost all his money and his house, and after much difficulty, he had now begun to stabilise his life a bit.

Yet he looked quite content with his life right now, and I guess the humbling experience of losing all your possessions and source of income must be a huge jolt to the ego and can make or break a person, depending on how one sees it and reacts to it. Mr Segal certainly didn't seem too fazed about his predicament, and he would come in regularly where we would have some deep philosophical discussions about life and how fate played such an important part in the direction of one's future path, yet we seem mostly unaware of what is actually happening to this mysterious destiny of circumstances.

Over the next few months, some unusual experiences began to happen as I began to lose interest in running my company with the once-ruthless control that I had and all the hours that I devoted to it. I began to feel like I had built a fortress around me with the rented warehouse and all the staff responsibilities. I was now trapped in a prison of my own making and wanting to get out! I was so distracted with things going on in my mind that were intruding into my thoughts more and more.

I was living in two different worlds at the same time. I still heard voices that spoke to me in a way that bypasses language. They were more like thoughts that entered me directly, but not vague or meaningless. They had power and more meaning than idle thoughts. Then one day while sitting at home on a quiet Sunday afternoon, I was staring at the small plant pot I had on my chest of drawers when all of a sudden, I saw the images of two small people sitting on the leaves. They were not moving but just sitting, looking out into the open space of the room. Yet they were not exactly lifeless as they seemed to vibrate with a soft energy of light.

I sat for a few minutes and I just observed them, trying not to move or take my eyes off them in case they disappeared. I could not keep my concentration up for too long and soon they faded and disappeared. During one of our interesting talks with Mr Segal, I told him of this phenomenal experience. He explained that, "Every living being has a guide that is always with them. This includes the animal kingdom, flora and fauna, as well as the minerals."

Children are often believed to have so-called imaginary friends that they talk to and sometimes see when they are alone and quite. These images are probably as real as the ones I saw that day. He went on to explain that "one of the brain's functions is to block access to phenomenal experiences of higher worlds. The brain doesn't produce consciousness but instead acts as a filter to higher consciousness, just as it acts as a filter for the endless barrage of sensual information and images that come at us, selecting only what we need to survive. But when we are in a different state of mind, i.e. more relaxed or even in crisis, the higher worlds miraculously tend to appear because our preoccupations and our logical mind are temporarily out of the way."

I remember reading Julian Huxley's book *The Doors of Perception* about his recognition that drugs have the effect of unblocking the filters of the mind. He experimented with Mescaline and had some profound experiences. The side effect is that it renders you incapable of being logical or productive. You become as a small child and your world as an adult would not be able to sustain itself. Drugs are like a quick trip to heaven and after the high, of course, you come 'crashing back to earth'. There are more natural ways to access the mind's phenomena without side effects.

However hard I tried, I could not repeat this vision again with those plants or any other, although some months later while doing an open-eyed meditation, I suddenly saw a face appear on the wall in front of me. It was an image of an old Chinese man who was looking straight towards me yet not staring at me. Could this be my inner guide? Could this be Mr Lee or at least the ghostly image of him? A few days later I was given a book by a friend to read. It was the *Tao Te Ching* by Chinese philosopher Lao Tzu. The universe seemed to be dropping small treasures in my path.

It is a series of 81 verses written in ancient Eastern philosophy. It became a close companion of mine for many years, and I still read it to this day because of the wisdom and humorous paradox it is written with. It teaches mainly about 'wu-wei', meaning, non-action or letting go, and how, by allowing things to take their own course, all is achieved, as interfering in a process often leads to confusion and chaos. His teachings have come in handy many times in my life over the years.

Of course, this went totally against my Western idea of logical thought, being in control, and making things happen by a determined effort. His teachings seem to be a form of reverse psychology. For instance, "If you want something, first let it go. If you want to get rid of something, first let it flourish." In comparison, the Bible states, "By giving you shall receive."

Basically, the message appeared to be, 'to only act under divine instruction'. But now I fought with all these new ideas I was contemplating. How could I possibly delete my 40 years of a belief system just like that? My resistance was high, yet I knew I now had to view this new period of my life with an open mind because my old rigid way of life had led me to near collapse.

I could at least review all new beliefs before allowing them into the temple of my mind. Some would have to be mulled over time and time again and some would have to be removed, screaming with resistance. Time was on my side for now at least. However, it was a time of much confusion and anxiety along with periods of peace and happiness in between. Reaching a happy medium was rarely achieved, and it was either one extreme or the other.

This way of life was not the escape that many people believed it was. In fact, it was the opposite as the disciplined responsibility weighed heavily on me compared to my previous carefree, over-indulgent lifestyle. Feeling like an 'Outsider' now and trying to live in the world yet not of it was a constant feeling of anxiety and feeling misunderstood in a world that doesn't care or at the very least, doesn't see you.

Jean Auel, who wrote *The Clan of the Cave Bears* series, tells of the main character and the heroine 'Ayla', who is raised by the now-extinct human tribe of 'Neanderthals' from the ice age, after they find her alone as a small child separated from her family of birth, who had died in an earthquake. She was from the more evolved human tribe of 'Palaeolithic man' that also roamed the plains at the same time and who we have now evolved from.

However, they tried to raise her as their own, yet she was in constant conflict with her adopted group of primate subspecies because their customs and way of life were too draconian and restricting on her more evolved psyche, with its greater sense of freedom and expression. Women held a very subservient existence in the Neanderthals' culture and were forbidden to hunt or learn to use weapons. They were forced to stay home and look after the cave and raise children while the men went hunting for days at a time.

Due to the frustration of her creative urge, she would secretly practice her hunting skills with the use of a sling and spear. As soon as she was adult and strong enough to survive on her own in the harsh deserts and ice plateaus, she abandoned the life she had adopted and left the tribe in search of her own people that she craved to reconnect with and be understood. After leaving, she spends lots of time surviving in the harsh world of predators and other obstacles that threaten her existence, just to be recognised for who she was. She does eventually find her own people.

This story is similar to the dilemma of the 'Outsider' who is like a spiritual tramp in the deserts of the psyche, feeling alone and like a wandering soul looking to be 'seen' and connect with those who are like-minded and more evolved.

My clothing company did eventually collapse, and I went out of business. I owed money to suppliers and the inland revenue for taxes unpaid. I lost my house and car, and owed money to the banks as well. My world had turned upside down. A friend put me up for a short while, and another gave me work for a short time too, while I tried to reorganise my life.

That's when I met Mr Segal again, who just like mysterious Mr Lee, would reappear. This time it was some months after my business had folded, and I had to move out of my house due to the lack of funds to maintain it. He appeared while I was at a demonstration on healing, being given by an Indian shaman from North America. I had already begun to see the fatal connection we had with the ending of our respective businesses. But had Mr Segal really come to prophesy the inevitable back then when we met? I never bluntly asked him because deep down I knew there was something about him that was beyond logical understanding. Was he for real, or was I imagining things about him? I couldn't get my head round it most of the time.

Over the next few years, our paths would keep meeting, more by chance than anything else. Although he would maintain that nothing in the universe happens by chance. "Nothing obscures anything else" was the way he put it, and he would remind me whenever I questioned why such difficulties were in my life. Anyway, we talked about the mysteries of life and why fate seemed to play a big part in our lives. And did we really have much control? He said, "an accident or crisis is neatly planned." Of course, they could be avoided if we were awake enough in the present moment, because there are usually warning signs in advance, but we tend to ignore them.

They appear as smaller incidents in our everyday lives and gradually increase into larger ones if we refuse to heed the warning that something is amiss. They increase into larger-scale crises, forcing us to wake up and smell the roses and follow the journey that destiny has mapped out for us. When we do take that first step on the road to 'awakefulness', then life tends to flow with more ease in a synchronised succession of events, until we feel we are being guided by the 'Higher Self' which connects us to the greater universe and all humanity that is and ever was!

Mr Segal said, "Each one of us is like an uncut diamond waiting to be found. Within us is a sparkle that remains embedded, yet has the potential to shine with multifaceted sides once we cut away the dross and polish it to reveal the multi-dimensional authentic 'Self', indestructible and with true beauty like the 'pearl of a great price'."

Then he would go off as mysteriously as he appeared. He reminded me of the Reluctant Messiah in the book *Illusions* by Richard Bach. The main character 'Joe' wandered around the mid-west of North America in a small biplane like a nomad with no direction, yet he was a qualified engine mechanic with the wisdom of a sage.

Chapter 8
The Dark Side

I did also discuss my situation with Mr Lee the next time we met, as I began to ask him many questions that were building up in my mind. His knowledge and experience on the mysteries led me to believe he, like Mr Segal, was indeed an enlightened guide, although he would never reveal himself, but often repeated a verse from ancient wisdom from the many past masters. Again, by Lao Tzu, he quoted:

He who talks doesn't know.
He who knows doesn't talk.

Then why am I such a blabbermouth?

I continued to study the *Tao Te Ching*, which gave me a great source of relief from the loss of my possessions and my shattered ego, because this ancient script values the wisdom gained in humility from loss of the overinflated ego and its pride in its success of gaining more information and possessions.

"The clever man seeks to add something more every day, yet the wise man lets go of something every day."

Mr Lee would quote from *Lao Tzu*.

Again, the message I was getting was about detachment and letting go. When I tried to pin him down to a question about what was likely to happen in my life in the near future, he would simply tell me to "wait and the answer would reveal itself. If the path you are on has 'heart' then chances are it's the right path." Patience was one of the lessons I had worked out on my own, as it was anxiety that always seemed to be the cause of most of my struggles. I drifted in and out of part-time jobs for a short period while I tried to make sense of what was happening to my life. I began going to different people for help: psychologists, motivational speakers, Buddhist meditation centres, different religious gatherings, talks on a wide range of subjects about the mysteries, etc. I needed this distraction because I knew something was going on. But somehow I realised this was not going to be a quick fix situation and I could be in it for the long haul. I often wandered around the city walking great distances just trying to get through the long days alone. I didn't know it then, but these periods of introspection were my attempt to find myself. To be honest, I had spent my whole life running as fast as I could in this rat race just to keep my head above water to avoid this 'very' confrontation. Isn't that why there are so many distractions and addictions we tend to fall into? "When one addiction is over another soon takes its place." Buddha was horrified when he first realised this notion! Substances like alcohol and any other distraction only serves to numb the senses and therefore numb the pain and loneliness of abandonment. The archetype of the 'Orphan' is deeply seated in the collective unconscious of the human psyche, and at some point we all feel abandoned as we try to cut a path through the growth of the society we live in. All this comes with being born into this incarnation and is the very thing that eventually brings us face to face with 'ourselves'. Without connecting and remembering who we are, we will always feel like orphans here on earth. Everything is born of frustration! Therefore, 'all is good'! As it says in the Bible when god created heaven and earth.

We have to face our dark side to see the light and know the 'higher self'. In the Kabbalah and the 'Tree of Life', the 'higher self' is represented by the sun and the ego is represented by the moon. And like the moon, the ego has no light of its own as the sun serves to reflect on its light side, leaving the dark side untouched. Therefore, we build multiple personalities to protect the dark side of the 'ego/moon' from being exposed. Once you seek the 'truth' and travel the path of honesty towards a more authentic life with greater awareness, then inevitably the dark side will present itself and your ego will be challenged, leaving your greatest fears exposed. This process is necessary to reach the 'Higher Self/Sun', which is the true source of light/higher consciousness.

Chapter 9
Moving On

Somehow I needed to find a way to keep on working on my 'self'; otherwise, I felt that I would slip back into the old routine, and old habits were lurking in the corners of my mind, almost waiting to resurface. Personality traits are etched into your psyche like engravings set in ancient stone. I needed a direction, a belief system that I could follow. I felt that I needed a support group because working with others gives some perspective on where you are at and avoids the dangers of delusions of grandeur and spiritual arrogance. But I did not want to join any religion that might stifle my creative freedom, even though I had gained so much from the ancient scriptures of books like the *Bible*, *Bhagavad Gita*, *Tao Te Ching*, etc. The journey was far from over, and in actual fact, it had only just begun. I was determined to delve into the mysteries, so I joined a psychotherapy workshop group that was being run by a psychologist who had trained in psycho drama, rebirthing, Reichian therapy breathwork, and also in 'Family Constellations'.

The first group session was particularly difficult, as I was reluctant to let go and join in with what I felt were pointless exercises, until I realised that it was my old arrogance that was holding me back from any likely progress in self-development. I had to break through the rigid beliefs that prevented me from having an open mind, letting go, and enjoying just being in the moment, whatever the outcome. Eventually, I was able to participate and go along with the humbling exercises we went through without judging or worrying about being judged.

Besides, we were all in the same boat, all trying to find a way to live that felt like we were progressing. I read once that George Gurdjieff, the popular Armenian mystic who was running a spiritual group in Paris in the early nineteen hundreds, had attracted a lot of wealthy people and well-known actors, especially from America, to some of his courses. The first thing he would do on day one of his course was to get them to go out into the garden and dig up huge holes in the ground and then fill them in again. The reaction of some of them was that "they had come to learn about his teachings of wisdom and philosophy and were not here for manual labour," to which he always replied that "your first lesson was to humble yourselves until you can develop an open mind."

In the group, we also worked on any past traumas that were likely to still be restricting our movement in living the best life we could. The Reichian breathwork was something that seemed to shift my old self into a new lease of energy. During this exercise, we all lay flat on the floor, covered with a blanket, breathing as heavy as possible for about an hour along with some powerful music. This causes hyperventilation, a sort of trance state that makes the body tingle all over and it seems to release pent-up stresses and causes a kind of rebirth where the body and even the psyche feels renewed and revitalised.

Many of the African tribes do ceremonial dancing to the beat of drums to whip them up into this same trance state. The Sufi Dervishes do a twirling dance to repetitive drum music. The American Indians and the Australian Aboriginals dance around a fire with their bodies painted, again to reach the same effect. Along with meditation, I was feeling more relaxed and less stressed in my everyday life at work and with social events.

Then I was introduced to 'Family Constellations', which was a system of reconnecting with past events by playing out a family scene in drama, having the other members of the group as actors who will play members of your family or your close friends. Someone else will even be selected to play your own part as the lead actor in this drama of your past as this is all about you. It was founded by Bert Hellinger, a German priest living in Zululand among the local tribes that still live a very basic existence and who greatly value family and especially their ancestors.

The chosen members of the said drama are called upon by the counsellor to speak up about the past event that they have selected to concentrate on. These events more often than not go back to childhood, which is when the personality is developed or in many cases that development is blocked by any particular incidents that occurred and were not resolved. Somehow, by a sort of telepathy, the actors will often recall important emotions or words that were relevant at the time that a past incident was unfolding, and the main subject of the drama (which is yourself) will just observe, as important events or traumas are played out and relived and hopefully some sense of clarity or closure will be achieved.

It is amazing to see how we are all interconnected in a oneness that remembers all past events. This certainly helps us to go back in time and recall incidents that have not been resolved and therefore allow us to move forward along our path of self-development as an individual and ultimately as a whole, so evolution can then progress to higher states of consciousness and finally 'paradise on earth'. "As above, so below." Each one of us makes up the whole and we only need to work on our own selves. Gandhi said, "be the change you want to see." Change does, however, cause disruptions in everyday life, with finding yourself in careers that no longer serve and relationships that may be stale and out of date. Change is literally the only constant. It brings on more experience with deeper insight into a working situation or a greater connection to meaningful relationships and higher states of awareness.

I had now begun to have the urge to travel to the most remote places that I could think of, and that was through the many relatively undeveloped countries towards and including East Africa. Often, when searching for the self, there is an urge to travel to remote and far-off places and just wander in no man's land and get away from normality. A spiritual journey often takes on the physical in the search for enlightenment. Also, it felt like I needed to be in a state of movement and adventure after many years of being bound to a stable life of work and family. Movement seems to free the shackles of the soul!

The story of the 'Wandering Jew' is one example. There are certain nomadic tribes that traditionally send their adolescent children out into the wild to survive for a period of time (usually a month or two), but this time has no definite time limit. It depends on when the individual is ready to return. The aim is a kind of initiation into adulthood where the initiate has to learn to survive on their own, and during this lone journey, it often serves to awaken the higher self because of the introspection that it causes and from the fear of being thrown out of the comfort zone and security which family life brings.

The Aboriginals in the Australian outback call this adventure the 'walkabout' where they wander the bush and deserts learning to survive in nature. The Masai of Tanzania and Kenya have a similar tradition where they were expected to hunt and kill a lion during this 'safari'. (Killing the lion is no longer practised because of obvious conservation reasons). Many young adult Westerners seem to have this same urge to leave their ancestral homes and roam different parts of the world in search of freedom.

"Finding your soul is more about getting off the path. That's where freedom lies. Do not follow where the path may lead but take the road where there is no path, and then leave a trail," words from a Foreign Legion soldier. India is a common destination, maybe because of its ancient spiritual connections. Africa is also a popular destination too because it is relatively undeveloped and its simplicity tends to bring one back to basics.

There are many young and some not so young who travel these paths. Travel strips away the daily routine and shakes away that futile existence many people feel in modern society. Deprived of the usual settings, it reduces you to being more open to curiosity, spontaneity and to love at first sight.

I met a Canadian woman backpacking through the many rural areas of East and Southern Africa. She was in her late 50s and told me that she was now free from family ties and also recently divorced, searching for adventure and to have a break from the modern world. This is what I could relate to as I was on the same quest and on my way to visit the nomadic Masai tribes of Tanzania.

To get there from South Africa, when you are travelling by road it requires travelling through four other countries. Each one of them is fairly vast with plenty of open spaces, game reserves and rural villages. Apart from the large towns and cities, the locals survive with only the basic essentials and mostly with no running water or electricity. Tanzania was probably the most untouched by tourism and modern technology that I went through.

The majority of the population survive through subsistence farming. The clothes they wore had holes that sometimes looked more like rags and most of them were barefoot. Their houses were usually made of mud and branches, with cramped living conditions, cooking on open fires which were mostly outside and on the ground. However, they had a curious and friendly welcome to such strange travellers from other parts of the world.

They lacked the technology that has saturated our senses with information in a culture of instant gratification. We in the Western world often seek to escape our dilemma to revive us, and it seems that they would give an arm and a leg for our lifestyles. So our paths cross without mutual understanding, but that is what creates our mutual curiosity.

The underlying need of these treks and journeys seems to be to go back to traditional living and just be in nature where we might feel more at home, away from this 'fast-paced' lifestyle we have inherited. During my short stay with the Masai, I slept in a mud hut and was treated like a special guest where they waited on me like a king. This is quite common in most parts of Africa, especially in the rural areas where they are more welcoming.

The children have big bright eyes and are fascinated by Westerners, sometimes touching my hair or wanting to stroke my arm because they had never seen a white man before.

Among the Masai, I was invited to an initiation that was taking place out in the bush in a secluded valley. There were about 12 young men who are called the 'Moroni', meaning warriors. Their hair is grown long in braided strands that are then rubbed with red ochre and oil, as well as their faces and most of their body. They wear a red cloth slung over their shoulder much like an ancient Roman soldier, and their red hair resembles the Roman helmet with red on top. Red, of course, was favoured by warriors because during battle it is more frightening to see an army approaching all in red.

This was their initiation ceremony into adulthood after they have finished their 'walkabout', from which they are given greater privileges, like being able to choose a bride and own cattle, etc. During the ceremony, a bull is slaughtered and the meat is cut into strips and cooked on an open fire. The young women participate by dancing and chanting and are dressed in colourful beading on their heads and around their necks, wrists, and ankles with brightly coloured clothes wrapped around them.

The whole event is conducted by their Sangoma (Shaman), who is their spiritual healer, herbalist, and chosen head of the tribe. He is distinguished by wearing a black cap, and he holds a baton with the strands of hair from an animal's tail. During the initiation, the warriors have to do a pogo dance, which is high jumping up and down on the spot until they reach exhaustion and then slip into a trance. Afterwards, they are cared for by the elders of the group until they come round after a few minutes. The warriors then have their long red locks completely shaved, signifying their transition into adulthood. From now on, they never allow their hair to grow long again. The whole ceremony is then ended by feasting on the roasted meat, drinking the blood, and also drinking a kind of homemade beer that looks more like a thick soup.

What seems fascinating is the similarities in worship that are practised around the world and makes you realise that we truly do all belong the same human tribe. We ultimately seem to have the same directions of personal growth and understanding, even if there are disturbances and disruptions along the way like war, crime, and struggles for survival. Evolution gives us a purpose!

Chapter 10
Who Am I?

My name is George Dexton, of that I'm sure, because it is written on my birth certificate that way. But who I am now and the kind of life I've led is a little hazy because the distant past feels unreal. I remember a lot of details that made up my past life, but I know I'm not the person I used to be. The philosopher Hegel wrote, "*The consciousness of self results in the interaction with others. By recognising person 'b' as a self-conscious being, we infer they must recognise the same in ourselves.*" So who I am now is more of an 'idea' from what I have gleamed from others. "We become who we are by our relationship to the environment in which we find ourselves." So in this incarnation, maybe I have been through different metamorphosis as I have grown up. Besides, we seem to always have a warped sense of 'self' as the philosopher Alan Watts stated, "the 'self' can't fully know 'itself', as a scabbard cannot slice through itself. Just as the eye cannot see its own eye or the teeth cannot bite their own teeth," and so the mind cannot fully comprehend its own mind. So who am I? I am nature, I am life, I am one with all. I am that I am. I am consciousness. 'I am aware that I am aware'. "I think therefore I am," proclaimed Descartes. The

Bible says "to Know the truth will set you free." Presumably, 'the truth of who I am'. But free from what? I know I've been searching for something all of my life but up until recently I wasn't even aware of it. Now I know it is this mythical or mystical 'freedom'. This search induces a feeling of hope and excitement and as a result, I feel more alive. It feels like I'm onto something! But like a blind man, I cannot grasp the whole picture but have only touched on parts of the whole and attempted to make up the rest in my imagination, like I was reading someone else's biography and used my imagination to imagine what it was like being that person or what that person was really like. Yet it's my life that I'm trying to fathom out here and it is not so simple because throughout all ages the mind has baffled all who have cared to delve into the dark recesses of the psyche and the collective unconscious with its unfathomable depths. The very first line of the ancient Chinese 'Tao Te Ching' states that:

The Tao that can be told
is not the eternal Tao.
The name that can be named
is not the eternal name.
Darkness within darkness
the gateway to all understanding.

But like any one of us, I've been on a journey through life that has triggered my imagination and has seemed to divide my past into different stages. I feel like I've lived three different lifetimes in this one incarnation. But can these memories of my past just be dreams of the 'self' that has travelled through time and space in different realms, and now has ended up in a higher state of consciousness and a less physical dimension with memories of my past once lived in a more mundane existence, like the animal world which we are undoubtedly a part of. In 'The Heart of Darkness' written by Joseph Conrad, he says, "No explanation can convey the very essence of a dream, and also no description of one's life experiences. We are all alone."

I know my thoughts are not dependant on matter, and so I'm not exactly definable, and so my body is not exactly who I am, and it will be discarded at my demise at the end of this incarnation. Is the world just all in my mind then? Right now, I'm simply here with fuzzy awareness, like muddy water. My body is possibly a creation of who I think I am, like a painting is not the artist but only their expression or impression of the artist. Therefore, like all of us, I am one with the creator, a spark of the divine!

But then, at my demise, I presume that all that will be left is my consciousness at its present level. Am I just an invisible memory bank then and what was the point of it all? These events and exercises that I can remember in the mundane world will presumably fade and die out eventually. I believe that in the timeless and formless spirit realms, the past and future blend into the present and so it is not restricted by matter. Consciousness is the basis of all that exists, yet it is so close to home that it seems forever beyond our reach.

However, in human form, once we have raised our consciousness to some higher level, we then have the ability to live in different realms because we are multi-dimensional creatures. But until then, the physical universe may be like an illusion, and we are being manipulated by the cosmic consciousness, and as observers, we on earth are being directed to see images designed to train us for the greater good. None of us then are here by accident, and every detail seems neatly planned. The universe appears to be an intelligent, well-constructed organism where nothing is random and all events are connected to make up the 'whole'. Something is going on beneath the surface of everyday life! Some other process is operating behind the scenes! If you can 'awaken' to this, it gives you the sense of 'wholeness', and you become sure there is a cosmic purpose.

Yet all these thoughts are causing me much dilemma now because I feel distant from the people around me. A kind of detachment that separates one from the crowd and the herd mentality that binds all humans in a kind of brotherly/sisterly oneness. Herman Hesse's 'Steppenwolf' is the character that comes to mind. Harry Haller is the tormented hero of the novel. He is constantly struggling with the dual personalities within him. The mundane beast/wolf tendencies that rise up from time to time against the spiritual aspect of himself, causing a kind of schizophrenia that makes him suicidal. The beast in him is always seeking pleasure of the flesh but the thin glazed coating of the human bourgeois conscience in him constantly seeks the balance of security and respect. He lives in torment as the tendencies of the beast in him are always denied by the judgemental human that wells up in him like a wave of guilt and self-loathing, making him feel empty inside. He becomes a shell of a person without a spine, much like a beetle with its innards of juicy mush held together by its thin, brittle coating. He constantly seeks freedom from his dilemma, but the freedom of independence has a price, and it becomes a curse, so he stands alone in society with the wolf howling at his heals. Guilt is the constant companion that drives him into more solitude and the loneliness of the 'Outsider'.

However much I strive to discipline myself towards a better life, the old me eventually comes back screaming and kicking just to be seen and recognised. The body resists change at every twist and turn in the journey to rid oneself of mother nature's pull, which only serves to keep you in step with the rest of the herd, to ensure the survival of the planet. So stepping 'out on a limb' then, is like swimming upstream against the torrent. The torrent of the human super ego that carries with it judgement from the universal traditions and customs of all cultures throughout all time.

The 'Lone Wolf' who runs against the pack has had to endure the wrath of the society in which he has incarnated into. Like the 'Romantics' of the 19th century, they see too deep and are therefore separated from the mainstream of the universal human psyche, left to wander in the desert like a spiritual tramp searching for other like-minded lost souls. These periods of torment known as 'the dark night of the soul' only serve to cement the determination to go it alone again until there comes a point of no return and now the only way forward is to attempt to survive and play along by acting out the life of an 'Insider' right here in the present, while remaining outsider, with no escapes or delusions of grandeur.

"Live in this world but not of it," said Christ. Hermann Hesse goes on to say, "The strongest of Outsiders like Harry Haller always force their way through the atmosphere of the bourgeoisie and into the cosmic consciousness." They are looked upon as legends and are often worshipped as gods. We should remember who we are? Christ said, "why callest me good, Ye will do greater things than I." Are we then not all

'Gods'? To know these truths takes great courage and inspires with the power to dream. Be still then looking at 'truth' in the face leaves you standing on the edge of a vast precipice with all your vulnerabilities rising to the surface.

The discipline to stay awake and be mindful of these beliefs takes a lifetime of struggle because the seeker can no longer live by the sweat of the brow like 'natural man' who lives for comfort and security amassing possessions and status to satisfy the ego, for they believe their life is the 'truth' but know not that they live in the lie. Whereas the awakened 'superhuman' lives submerged in the truth and cares less for the things of the mundane world because they have built themselves higher worlds to move in at will and yet they strive to remain earthed, moving up and down the ladder with their feet on the ground. They are not just legends and messiahs from the distant past but are present here and now; otherwise, the world would fall into chaos and destruction.

To live out your destiny is to live a life of purpose, for a man without a purpose has the weight of his mind to carry. The masses of the world could argue that theirs is not to rise up and see the light because the standard set by the messiah's of the past is simply beyond the natural man, whose only possibility in this incarnation is to survive and hopefully raise the next generation to live a more prosperous existence than their forefathers without the hardships of poverty and lack but still without much thought in their heads; they are like the blind leading the blind.

However, each one of us has unlimited potential to break out from the darkness. "In the country of the blind, the man with one eye is king," wrote George Bernard Shaw. It is not for the faint-hearted or even the average bourgeois to seek out the way of the spirit and break through the illusions of the physical world. The time will come when each one will open up like a flower and turn towards the sun in search of the light that calls the soul to take the journey homeward bound on a path of self-discovery. The work goes on.

Until that veil is drawn, then evolution will slowly move on with the few awakened souls who keep the eternal torch alight as a beacon to any seekers that emerge from the debris left by the gold rush of the material world by those who have sought to clothe themselves with possessions to avoid confrontation with the naked truth of who they actually are!

Each one of us is free to follow their own path because the truth lies in the individual and no one religion can fit into all. Truth is not an idea; you have to feel it! The Danish philosopher Kierkegaard stated that 'Truth is Subjective'. Individuality depends on listening to your intuition and finding what is right for you, using the power of the scriptures and from all the wisdom that is inherited from our ancestors and fitting into a mixing pot of your own, for each path is unique.

Individuality leaves you living on the edge of society but if you are not living on the edge, you are taking up too much room!

Chapter 11
Future Islands

I had heard many stories about the mystical *Future Islands*. Some say they got this name because they are a myth and don't exist and some say it's because it is beyond the world of mundane existence. Either way, there is very little known about this archipelago because those who have visited seem reluctant to reveal their experience about the place for some reason. Some say it is a kind of Utopia that arose many centuries ago and has remained virtually untouched throughout the world's history of conflict and invasions and even during the two great wars of the last century. It all adds to the mystery of the place.

Access to the islands requires no visa or other restrictions, so anyone is welcome without prejudice. However, it only tends to attract those who are interested in a mystical life of wonder and intrigue. It would not appeal to the annual 'package holiday' tourist or the simple pleasure sun seeker, and although the weather is ideal, the place has not been set up to accommodate this kind of visitor.

So now I was on board this ship heading out towards this mysterious archipelago' in the Atlantic Ocean. The weather was calm with just a slight breeze, and a turquoise blue sea was shimmering in the sun. The faint rumble of the engine was the only sound as I was heading to a chance to step into another realm, having been to the initiation ceremony back home where I was invited to join in this trip to the islands along with some of the other initiates and many other old souls who had made this pilgrimage regularly.

I saw someone who looked familiar. It turned out to be Cecille, who was on my Awakening course, and we chatted about the course and how it had affected our life since. She was dressed in black with a petite figure but with a dynamic presence. She had strawberry blonde straight hair, shoulder-length, and with white pearlescent skin. Sparkling blue eyes with an open face and fairly ordinary features except for a cute dimple on the left side of her fresh, vibrant mouth that altogether I found quite attractive.

She was softly spoken and somewhat more focused than the last time I saw her. She appeared more confident now, but it was more an air of acceptance about her as though she had gone through some sort of transformation. I found it difficult to look into her eyes at first, maybe because I could sense she could see through me, yet I found her easy to get on with, and so we stuck together a lot of the journey, sometimes in silence which I took as a sign of true friendship.

The ship eventually docked in the busy harbour surrounded by huge commercial buildings that were brilliantly white and in pristine condition. There were people meandering about the wide streets where there was little traffic and little noise because all the vehicles were electric and fossil fuels in general were a thing of the past. Everyone seemed to be quietly moving with a sense of purpose yet they were sort of detached, each with their own path of direction.

It was like watching a scene from a silent movie in a land and culture devoid of emotion yet the atmosphere was quite peaceful.

We all disembarked and were guided to a bus that was to take us to our accommodation and to meet our point of contact, who was a sort of guide or mentor while we were staying on the islands. Her name was Seri, and she was a well-groomed, with dark hair and bright brown eyes. Although she was of average height, she had a large presence and appeared somewhat serious with a strong personality. Seri informed us that there would be a short introduction now, and we all gathered into small hall to listen. She started by telling us why there was so much controversy about the islands, and she did not try to defend or justify it.

She explained, "The islands have a unique system of politics unlike any other country, that brings a feeling of release from the inhibiting laws of the rest of the world. In the Western world, their ideals that have become a bourgeois compromises called democracy. Democracy seems to be lusted over, more for the word than the reality of it! Then of course you have 'Socialism' with its sharing of misery and its pitiful handouts to the needy, which seeks to keep the masses down in a state of ignorant bliss, where any attempt of individuals rising up to realise their unique power and wealth is quashed in condemnation. Altogether these policies cause a futile existence in most people and inhibit the sense of adventure that life was surely meant to be."

She went on, "Here on these islands, free enterprise is greatly encouraged with low taxes and little or no interference from government on monopolies or censorships. If you try to stifle a free market, you create a black one." The islands are a tax haven for many rich foreigners as the local banks offer hidden accounts for greater privacy.

There is no social security system here, although there are private welfare organisations that rely on 'genuine' charity from the public to ease the burden of the misplaced or fallen. Charity can only work if it is voluntary. It should come from the heart, and each individual should be at liberty to give only when the time is right for them to give and not from pity or guilt, as these are negative energies. Nor from pressure from governments who forcefully raise taxes to hand out benefits at their own discretion.

Forcing people to hand out their hard-earned cash is counterproductive because it does not carry the vital energy that is created through compassion, which is just as important to the giver as to the benefactor. Charity should be more of a temporary hand-up rather than a handout that often has no ending. It takes away your dignity when you have to rely on aid, and then you become a slave to your donor, more and more dependent in a never-ending downward spiral.

Just look at all the third world countries that are dependent on foreign aid from the Western world, which has attempted to enable them but only served to do the opposite, and they have slipped further into a state of hopelessness and self-pity. Looking at the poorer countries of Africa, it would appear that most aid is harmful. The billions of dollars of Western aid that have been handed out in recent decades have caused a culture of dependency, discouraged investment, and worst of all, tempted selfish corruption and brutal dictators lining their pockets, resulting in more hopelessness and less production.

Africa doesn't need charity. They need hope. They are generally hard-working people who need good, genuine leaders whose real motive is the welfare of the country! Dignity is the key to maintaining hope.

There are no restrictions on euthanasia here. All drugs are legalised, and there are no extradition agreements with the rest of the world.

On religion, the freedom of choice is vital, and there are many different religious groups operating without prejudice. However, it is believed that wealth and success are great motivators for genuine seekers of the truth. Religious groups that promote piety through lack and struggle do not thrive here. "If you want to try to convince a rich man that God exists, then you need to have at least as much money as him!" Capitalism is greatly encouraged rather than being frowned upon because without money, you cannot help anyone, and therefore, it seems selfish to limit yourself to just your own needs!

Try to make people happy and you lay the groundwork for misery.

Try to make people moral and you lay the groundwork for vice.

Try to make people secure and you lay the groundwork for sloth.

Therefore, let go of all desire for the common good, and the good becomes common as grass.

Tao Te Ching.

The islands always remain neutral in a time of war and have no arms or weapons for defence. The more defences you amass, the more prone to attack you become! The police keep a low profile here, and punishments are minimal, believing there is no evidence that brutal force is a deterrent as it is more likely to be met with stronger resistance. The more law enforcers you deploy, the more criminals will appear. "For every action, there is an equal and opposite reaction." The concept of these unusual levels of relaxation is believed to be a form of reverse psychology where nothing is right or wrong. It's only what you think it is! In the Bible, it states, "Do not eat from the tree of the knowledge of good or evil." This is the first sin.

The islands' politics have been labelled as an extreme form of capitalism and have caused a lot of controversy with the rest of the world, especially with activist groups who put their anger into what they believe is a good cause but know not that it only serves to increase the toxic energy released into the atmosphere. Where's the sense in that? Because of the 'law of entropy', chaos causes greater chaos and yet they think they are changing the world for the better. Surely loving or at least 'tolerating what is' is the best way to create change. You cannot 'fight for peace' that sentence alone goes against logic. However, loving what is, is not pretty, is a hard thing to do, but that may be the ultimate challenge. All these controversial ideas have only brought a greater level of intrigue to these mystical islands.

Then Seri asked if there were any questions, but the room was silent as people seemed to be trying to chew over what they had just heard! There would be other discussion groups during our brief stay where we would be told more about the kind of life here and the many benefits of this kind of existence and any questions would be answered.

After settling into my room, I wandered out into the streets alone and heard music in the distance, so I headed off towards the sound coming from a large park where there was a bandstand with a group of musicians quietly playing what sounded like the music to *MacArthur Park*, with a sprinkling of people who had stopped to listen. The park had a picturesque lake with white swans gliding on the calm waters, to the rhythm of the music. Further on, as I left the park, I walked along a wide boulevard lined with flowering Jacaranda trees in a swish of purple haze. Traffic cruised past at a steady pace, without much urgency.

I then entered a cafe where people were relaxing outside on the pavement terraces, sipping their drinks and chatting in holiday mode out in the midday sun. So I joined them to get some rest from the long walk and ordered a cool drink. As I sat there pondering about how life takes on such twists and turns and why things ebb and flow the way they do, I was so lost in thought that I hadn't noticed someone stood at my table. It was Cecille who greeted me with, "hello darling." I was a bit surprised by her intimate greeting, but then I remembered that she greeted most people with that phrase. She had changed into a cool white summer dress and looked fresh after our long journey by sea. She sat there next to me.

"You look so beautiful, within and without, like an angel." I never said that to her, but those were the words that kept running through my mind whenever I was in here presence. I talked to her for a while to try to get to know her more. I asked her, does she have children? Of course, that was a loaded question, but she didn't take the bait and just gave me a one-word answer. We agreed to take a walk the following day up towards the hills in the distance just outside the city. For now, we caught up on some of the past, and just being in her presence filled me with awe because of her delightful radiance that she exuded.

We met the next morning, and as we set off for the hills, we chatted about nothing in particular as we strolled through a wooded area where there were many kinds of plants, small animals, and birds. Here we bumped into our guide Seri, who said, "The flora and fauna are like the archetype of all manifestations that appear in our plant life back home." This is probably where they originate from in the creative world before manifesting on earth in the dense physical world we know of as mother nature. They seemed to have more vivid colours and more vibrant life in them. She asked, "Can you pick up on the energy here?"

I stood silently for a while. She went on, "We can all tap into this invisible type of energy. In medieval times before the industrial revolution, people relied on their intuition a lot more. They were more connected to an invisible force and to nature's natural laws. But somewhere along the line, it all changed. The scientific world was developing. People like Isaac Newton and others began to believe that the universe always operates in a predictable manner. Science became the dominant force, with a revolution in physics and technology. However, much later, Einstein's ideas were to change our then rigid thinking, claiming that hard matter is mostly empty space with a flow of energy running through it. Quantum physics looked at these energies on a more miniscule scale, breaking up small particles of this energy and observing how they react. They found even the act of observation altered the result. The basic blocks of the universe look like pure energy which is influenced by the expectations of the observer or experimenter. Everything is therefore relative, which goes against the old understanding of the workings and mechanics of the universe. For example, when you are in love, you become more present, then beauty strikes you deeper, and you begin to see shapes with more sharpness and colours become more vivid as if you can actually see them vibrating with life because they have an aura field around them."

I stopped to think about what she had said. Then I realised that actually this energy field has been known about for centuries because the ancient practice of the Chinese martial arts like karate, taekwondo, and tai chi talk about maintaining a balance between the mind, body, and heart, which then creates a fourth force known as 'Chi' energy. The ancient Christian saints might call this the 'Elixir of life'. Then she said, "Let's try an experiment. Let go of the mind's constant chattering and try to hold the mind still by focussing on a point within an object, like a tree trunk, for example. Hold your gaze and concentrate on that space. Then relax your gaze with your eyes slightly out of focus."

After a while, amazingly, I began to pick up glimpses of light and an aura became visible. It reminded me of a short poem by T.S. Eliot: 'There is only the point, the still small point'. If we can just stop the obsessive thinking process for a few moments at a time, then all becomes peaceful!

We said goodbye to Seri, and Cecille and I moved on. Eventually, we came to a clearing high up above the city in the beautiful mountain scenery. Shimmering streams meandered leisurely down through valleys, and then waterfalls cascaded dramatically into limpid pools, which created a mirage of the rising hills. We walked along a clifftop by the coastline for a while until we came across a small cove, and looking down into it, we saw a white sandy beach with a deep sea of turquoise translucent water. At first sight, it was breathtaking as we just stood in awe of the beautiful scenery. It was sublime, like a picture postcard. A faint steep path wound down into the cove, so after descending, we explored the far reaches of the bay. The sky was big and the sea was calm, which produced a peaceful and quiet influence. No thoughts of anxieties entered my mind, and just being in the present with Cecille and this little corner of 'paradise' was enough at this moment.

Then Cecille began to tell me a little about her life and how she came to be on the same 'Awakening course'. She had been brought up in a large industrial city in France in a very close and caring family. Yet, when she left business college, she was undecided about what career she wanted to pursue, and with no direction, she seemed to lack the ambition of most of her fellow students and friends. So, on a whim, she had followed an urge to see some of the more exotic places in the world and travelled to Africa to stay with an old school friend who came from the Belgian Congo, now the DR Congo. While staying there for a few months, she instinctively knew that her destiny involved some kind of natural healing work after she had visited a local tribe and witnessed the 'Sangoma' (traditional medicine man) performing hands-on healing and also the use of herbal medicine from plants found in the surrounding bush. Twenty years later and lots of tough times, she now has her own holistic practice and homeopathy. She has found some purpose in life now and says she has been on a journey of self-discovery ever since, and still the work goes on, which brings her to the islands. Only on looking back in retrospection can she now see how fate played its part, with a reason why she lacked drive in the corporate world of business and how it brought her out here to where she is at this moment in time and doing what she believed was her destiny. Schopenhauer had said, "That in old age and looking back over the past years, one can see a pattern of meaning, that their lives were not just random events but there seemed to have been a purpose that was ordered by a mysterious greater universe."

Cecille then turned to me and said in a casual tone, "So what is your purpose in life, George?" It took me by surprise because it was a subject that always struck me with self-doubt, and it was a question I had been avoiding for years. I had not wished to take it face on because I thought that it might be a cause of ridicule, or was I just afraid to commit to such a definite path? Commitment has always been an issue in my life, so I have often been told. Either way, I stumbled to give a decent answer, but just said it would most likely become apparent sooner or later!

The sun was now receding, so we ambled back up the rocky slopes and headed back down to the city. The following morning as I wake, I find it hard to concentrate on much but Cecille because I'm beginning to lose myself in her. Is this the feeling of love welling up in my mind, or is it more the effect of the islands on both of us? I'm a bit confused about what's going on. I'm not sure if this is a feeling of romance I have for Cecille or just the joy of life in these idyllic islands with someone like her. I try to assume the latter; otherwise, expectations will distract me from this experience and maybe even ruin this beautiful connection we have together. I decide to just be with what is and remember that timing is crucial, so for now, I just take things as they come and try not ruin the moment. I'm reminded of a verse by Lao Tzu in the *Tao Te Ching*, which states:

Fill your bowl to the brim and it will spill.
Keep sharpening your knife and it will blunt.
Care about people's approval and you will be their prisoner.
Do your work, then step back.
The only path to serenity.

During the day, we had some discussion groups to attend to. The topic today was, not surprisingly, about 'Being happy to be alone'. Seri explained that many people will often say they are happy being alone or that they don't need a partner and repeat it often to convince themselves it's true. Being truly alone does not always require solitude, as being independent can be with or without someone. This I know but still struggle at times with the paradoxical reality of it.

Then in the evening, I wander out alone to check out the night life in the laid-back atmosphere of the tropical islands. There are families out together wandering through the streets with no particular place to go but bonded as a group. There are some street stalls selling food and gifts crafted from the local community. There are the occasional bands playing music that wafts through the avenues and alleys in between. It feels like the holiday season, but I instinctively know it is like this throughout the year, here on the islands. Eventually, I head back and lay for a few hours in my room, daydreaming about how my life is developing into a more perspective train of thought and that I'm aware of my shifting emotions and how I feel in each different phase of change. Then I drift off to sleep and wake up late with my mind on Cecille again, and the beauty that I see in all her mannerisms. How, when she looks at me, I feel like a rabbit caught in the light of her gaze. Her voice was like a melody and would reach right inside of me and grab my most hidden emotions. I feel an erotic connection to her but this I know should not be confused with romantic or sexual feelings, as many people often do. 'Erotic energy' can be a deep feeling between two people whose lives are brought together by fate for various reasons, that may or may not be a romantic connection, but could be for an important work relationship or close friendship on a deeper level. It is not always romantic, and it can be ruined if mistaken for sexual energy. It can cause much confusion if an affair is played out in real life when this powerful energy has been misinterpreted. This kind of love is like an energy field that attracts and pulls you in when you are ready to be so open, that you connect deeply to the very energy of life itself. It feels like there is no way out of it and it would take a huge amount of effort to resist. So I try to contemplate what would happen if I just walked away from it, but I feel helpless to free myself from this kind of attraction. "The power of love is as strong as an atomic bomb." But I can't help wondering what this feeling is, because before I left for the islands I felt in control of my emotions to some extent at least. Now I feel like a surfer and I'm riding on the crest of a wave not knowing what the outcome will be. I can't even jump off the board because I feel bound to it by an invisible cord? So I just have to go along with the flow while it lasts! I feel in love and everything going on around me feels synchronised like dancers dancing in step. If this is how paradise is meant to be, then heaven and hell are surely just states of mind!

That night I dreamt of Cecille again. We were walking together in some unknown open place, and there she had told me that she had a partner, a lover who she lived with back in the big city. She tried to explain that it was possible to be in love with more than one person at a time, because there were different kinds of love. She was trying to tell me it was all right to feel this kind of love and to just let it flourish. Then I was woken and recalled the dream. It was disappointing to know that I may never have a romantic love relationship with her, yet there was a relief to know that the feelings I had for her were true and were reciprocated, yet there was no need to have any expectations from either of us. There is always an anxiety in romance because generally there is something to be gained or lost and it swings from high to deep, between paradise and perjury, sweet and sour! But in this deep erotic love, it is unconditional and there are 'no ties that bind'. True love is a release of emotions that sets you both free and causes the soul to soar out into 'all' space because the energy it brings is released into the universe for 'all' time.

The next morning as I woke, I began to contemplate how I would react to Cecille knowing what I know now, and indeed how she would react to me now that I felt more comfortable knowing our relationship had become clearer? I met her in the lobby soon after, and seeing her was just as it was before. The feelings generated between us were a deep stirring within my solar plexus area, and being in her presence was spellbinding. Yet I could now feel that this was platonic and therefore to just 'be with it'. We sat and chatted a bit and then went our separate ways for the day. So moving on from there, I realised that it was soon time to depart. I took a last walk around the town and went to the docks to see where all the shipping arrived. Mostly boats from the other islands as they quietly disembarked, and the people moved along on their way like ants going about their daily work, stopping to connect and then moving on again with the purpose of somewhere to go. I walked along the pier and the water was a clear bluey-green with tropical fish swimming about. Their bright colours catching the sun at different angles causing a rainbow of shimmering colours as they swam in unison like they were performing a well-rehearsed sequence. The water swells and dips in a constant rhythm like the pulse of a living organism. I gaze out into the endless sea for a while in deep contemplation.

Back at the hotel, there are people milling about the lobby as they are making plans to depart. After saying goodbye to Seri, we all eventually left for the docks where there is a huge liner waiting patiently, loaded and ready to begin its epic trek across the huge open seas. We moved off from the moorings and began to thread through the islands which were scattered like a myriad of fragments chipped away their mother gem. Then on towards the distant sea until the sight of the islands fades behind us. On board, I looked out to the vastness around me and I'm amazed at the distance our oceans of water have with the horizon stretching out in all directions, right across this panoramic expanse. Also, the vastness of sky above that goes on into all eternity. In this moment, I suddenly glimpse my connection to the 'oneness of all'! But here I stand on the edge of the universe and my body is just a speck of dust with just a short lifespan in the greater scheme of things. Again I wander who I am that inhabits this physical form with its five senses then fades and dies like a leaf withered by the seasons. What will become of me then? Will my soul then lose the separateness that it feels and then become one with all again? Or will I wander about in confusion without my body? Will I depart to far reaches in some parallel universe aeons away? Will I ever come back to this plane of life? Or will I just melt into the pool of the collective consciousness forever more?

Outside on the upper deck, I saw Cecille quietly sat in a deck chair looking out to sea, so I joined her and we ordered drinks. She told me that her journey to the islands had cleared up a lot of things that she had contemplated as a young child growing up in a large woodland property in a quite suburb where as an only child she would spend much of the time in a world of imagination, losing herself in thoughts and dreams of a perfect world with creatures and entities from other realms. Those times have always been a safe place to go to when she struggled with the harsh realities of life in 'Earth school', as she put it. She looked radiant as ever as she spoke more about her past, and I was surprised when she told me about her wild days of rebellion in her teenage years when she had rejected her upbringing and the stiff society expectations made on her by her family and community. She had wanted to leave home as soon as she finished school and seek a life of adventure and meaning but was prevented by her parents who insisted on her going to college, where she then got into a habit of binge drinking and a sexually promiscuous lifestyle with a dubious procession of so-called friends and acquaintances. All that had caused a lot of tension and trouble with her parents and the authorities at the time. She said she had still felt frustration with a strong rebellion welling up in her from time to time, but was now more mature to deal the dark energy in a more positive way and had few regrets about her past actions and her life of debauchery, because it had been the foundation for her quest for independence and individuality that she fought to achieve. I could see that she was more at peace than even before the visit to the islands, and maybe that was also because I felt more at ease with her now that this energy we together had become uncomplicated. We arrived at our destination in the evening and disembarked. Cecille and I agreed to keep in touch because there seemed to be something common about our journeys, and maybe we could share experiences with each other as we worked towards our futures. The purpose of our meeting did not feel like a random event, and maybe nothing in the universe ever happens by chance?

Chapter 12
The Wisdom of Insecurity

Soon, I decided on a complete career change and went to see a friend who was an estate agent, as I had often thought about selling houses in the past. Andy explained that the company he was working for would most likely take me on and train me without any experience because they never paid out any regular wages, as all money earned was on commission only. So there was not much risk on their part. The commission was basically 3% of the total price of any property that was sold. This sounded good at first, and so I had arranged an interview and was accepted on the spot. However, there was one slight drawback. After a short training period of a couple of weeks, I was told a sale would then take about four months to six months to complete from the time of the first acceptance of a sale up until the final completion of the transaction. At that point only, is when the money is transferred to the seller and only then would the commission be paid out to the estate agent via the seller. How was I going to survive that long? I had rent to pay, children in school, and food to provide. Plus, I had to do a lot of travelling to different properties and with clients to meet, and of course, I would have to sell a property pretty soon. I had no other options or offers coming my way, so I accepted and began training after borrowing a small amount of money to at least get me going for a couple of months or so. After the first month, I had done quite a lot of appointments and show days at different properties, but nothing was happening. I had no sales and no potential interested. I struggled on with lots of encouragement from my colleagues who kept saying 'fake it till you make it' but I was not good at bullshitting like the others, who used all the estate agent jargon that seemed to be essential to the trade, for example 'sparkling pool' even if it was murky green with algae. Also, 'stunning views' when it looked across the uniform city's suburbs. I once put in one of my adverts that was about to be published in the local weekly paper, a heading, 'Ordinary home for the ordinary family'. For this, I was called into the manager's office to explain my negative view. I said, "That was the only feeling that this very plain little house gave me." I was censored from then on until I could fabricate a rosy picture that was likely to attract at least a handful of potential buyers to the Sunday viewings. The area I was given was in a predominantly white suburb of upper-middle-class bourgeoisie. Very few blacks could afford these prices, although now that the apartheid regime was over, there was now a whole new market of potential buyers, and the banks had recognised this by granting mortgage loans without any deposit to first-time buyers, so the property market boomed for a few years. My first sale was to a middle-aged white lady who was recently divorced and looking to move into her own place. However, she backed out of the deal just before the transaction was completed, and I thought I had lost my first commission just as I was about to get paid. But as luck would have it, she had paid a ten percent deposit which she was made to forfeit, so I was able to get my full commission and soon thereafter was now selling enough at times to make a decent living. 'Uncertainty' was a constant companion in this type of career, but it did act as a stimulant!

However, I was bored with this type of clientele who I found were very superficial and dull, let alone materialistic, but what did I expect in the property market selling a commodity that was the biggest single purchase that clients were ever likely to make? It was not going to be the casual 'walk in the park' with like-minded souls searching for their little piece of paradise. But even that sounds too tedious. Yes, I knew these feelings were wrong because after all, I once was the one who had sought for more and more possessions thinking this would be the saviour of me. This experience had been exciting at one time, and now I had lost it all. For me, it was all overrated and gave a false sense of security and pride, because a mortgage loan is not exactly the same as owning a property. You are always a slave to the money lender! Yet for some reason, this was the career I had found myself embroiled in! There must be a lesson in here somewhere?

I struggled to keep up with the necessary conversation required to try to impress people and gather around me a bunch of hangers-on looking for that chance to own a piece of real estate in suburbia that would lift them up the social ladder and make them feel they 'had arrived'. So, without too much judgement, I persevered. Until I saw an advert from a small family-owned estate agent that wanted someone to sell and manage commercial buildings and residential blocks of flats in the inner city. These were areas that were now being deserted because of the crime rate that was spiralling in down town Johannesburg after the demise of the apartheid government. My first thought was that, "Who, if they had money, would want to buy in such a depressed market as this?" Let alone the crime rate! But I went along for an interview with a very enthusiastic Jewish man whose family had opened this estate agency back in the good old days of growth and prosperity after his grandfather had emigrated here from Eastern Europe after the 2nd World War. He explained that because the affluent property investors were now desperate to cut their losses and get out while they could, prices were so low that there was now a great many risk-takers who could afford to pay cash and who were making a fortune buying cheap, and then renting out to the working-class blacks that were flooding into the city from the rural parts of South Africa and from other African countries. Johannesburg is known to most Africans as 'Egoli' the Zulu term for 'City of Gold'. Some even believed that the city was 'paved in gold', and many flocked here looking for job prospects. So I accepted his offer and moved into an office in their company. It was in part of the inner city that was showing signs of decay, and very few whites would even venture into these parts, let alone come to work here five days a week. For me, it sounded like a step up from the mundane suburbia. It was tough at first because everybody kept giving me negative feedback about the prospects or lack of them. One incident was when a rich property owner who couldn't get his way with a deal I was trying to negotiate. He was asking me to do something which I considered unethical. So eventually he turned on me and shouted down the phone, calling me a "shitty little estate agent, selling shitty little houses, in a shitty little suburb." He might well have been right! But for some reason, and I can't quite figure it out even now, the whole episode seemed to motivate me even more and from then on I got over the fact that I had gone from selling luxury houses in plush areas to selling at the lowest end of the market in a potential slum. Basically, instead of climbing the corporate ladder in estate agency, I had descended it and ended up on the lowest rung. However, there was always something interesting happening here on this darker side of the street. 'Deeper into chaos', this was the real Africa that bought me here in the first place, even though it was a 'concrete jungle' that I ended up in! It seemed that danger and life-threatening situations were what I sought for some reason! "Nothing much is ever achieved through ease. It is the challenge of struggle that brings greatness," I remember reading this once. It was the adrenaline, I suppose, that was the motivating force, and like the many explorers of unknown parts of the world who seemed to have a death sentence over them, this was my adventure and what intrigued me. When I had first arrived in Johannesburg, I was often warned not to go into certain parts of the city's deprived areas or the black townships, but that only served to challenge me to go there even more. I felt that I was not exactly free if I are racked with fear!

On one occasion, I was asked by a landlord who had virtually given up on his seven-story office block deep in the city centre to try to find a buyer. It had been completely taken over by squatters, yet he wanted me to try and find a buyer to take on this hopeless situation at a knock-down price with non-paying tenants and all! So one morning, I went into the city centre to try and get a good look at the place. The building was right next to a large informal market where a vibrant, rowdy crowd was bustling through the arteries of the narrow streets. The main entrance was wide open, so I wandered in and began climbing the stairs, passing a few dishevelled-looking squatters on their way out, like cockroaches scurrying at the first sign of light. The place was dark and smoky with no electricity, and of course, there was no running water or sewage, so the stench of urine and excreta was rife in the early morning heat. When I got to the first-floor landing, it was virtually pitch black, and all I could see were the people's spot-round eyes like dominoes in their black faces. Each floor had been stripped clean of any fixtures and fittings. Even the partitioned walls of the offices were removed now, leaving just a large concrete floor space lined with mattresses and bedding. Cardboard and newspapers covering the light from the windows, with just a few rays of sun seeping through. Many people were still in bed at this time of the day, sleeping on the floor, looking so lifeless. It was sinister and spell bounding at the same time. The only thing that seemed to move were the flies. After a couple of floors, I had seen enough and turned back to leave. But as I got to the exit, there were now three suspicious-looking men, about 30 years old, loitering with intent. I greeted them and tried to pass, but one of them blocked my passage of escape and asked me what I wanted in there. I explained that I was sent by the owner to have a look because he was looking to sell. I began to feel pricks of sweat on my face, then trickling through my brow, and a feeling of absolute fear cursed through me. I let the feeling flow through my body without blocking it as I breathed deeply and tried to remain calm. The talkative member of the gang of three, who clearly was the leader and had a very cocksure attitude with a menacing look about him, told me that this building was not for sale and that it was their building now, so I should not be here. The other two slowly moved in on me, so with my heart now pounding from fear, I suddenly had a feeling of peace and calm come over me. With that, I found the courage to move off, and I managed to squeeze through a gap between them and then through a mass of people as I navigated my way along the pavements and then scrambled back into my car like a startled animal regaining its burrow. But as I got in, I sensed that one of them was right behind me, so I closed the door and locked it immediately. The ring leader was standing by my car door, and he motioned me to wind down the window. So, I wound it down a fraction, and at that point, we were face to face. Although I have probably never seen a murderer before, I was sure he had 'killed', because of the absolute terror in his eyes. Again, he mentioned again that I should not come back to this building, so I nodded as I wound up the window and drove off with relief that I had escaped with my life intact. When a building has been hijacked, it is normally controlled by a gang of drug dealers who then rent out mattress-sized floor space to many of the homeless city dwellers at a cheap daily rate. On each floor, there can be a few hundred sleeping side by side, and sometimes they even build homemade fires for cooking, right on the concrete floor. There was even an incident a few months later when a hijacked multistorey city centre office building had caught fire and went up in flames. Thirty to forty squatters were burnt alive in the scramble to get out.

A few weeks later, I was asked by a client if I could come to one of the black 'townships' to pick up an amputee who had been granted enough workman's compensation to be enable him to buy a small flat for himself. The accident that had left him crippled had occurred while driving a company car, and it had not been his fault. I set off early one morning to pick him up from 'Soweto', the largest township in Johannesburg. I was to take him to see some of the flats we had for sale. After driving into 'Soweto', eventually I managed to find his small place among the rows and rows of uniform government housing that were provided for the blacks during the apartheid era. The numbers on the houses were poorly marked, but luckily I spotted someone standing outside on crutches and rightly presumed that must be him. So I pulled up outside his house and got out to try and help him into the passenger seat. As I did this, three young, rough-looking men appeared and shouted something to my client in Zulu. With that a huge commotion erupted and then one of them pulled out a knife and held it to my chest, motioning me to get back in the driver's seat. They all got into the car too, leaving the cripple hobbling on the roadside. The one with the knife was now sitting next to me and told me to start the car as he now held the knife to the side of my neck. I started up, and we drove off as he began directing me further into the township. The tension with all of us inside this small space was extremely uncomfortable, and throughout the ordeal, I was imagining all sorts of terrible outcomes. But then, all of a sudden, a peaceful calm came over me, and I got to a point of not being stressed or even worried about the outcome. Maybe I sensed that even though I was in a life-threatening situation, no harm would come to me. Then the mood between all of them slowly became lighter, and they even joked with me about whether I wanted a lift back to Johannesburg. Soon, they stopped at a large intersection on the road and told me to get out before relieving me of my wallet that had only a few rand in it! Here I was, a white man in a suit wandering around and lost in a black township, getting some strange looks until some very kind family stopped to pick me up and gave me a lift back to my offices. About a week later, the police called me on the phone to say they had recovered my vehicle. I was then asked to come to the police station for an identity parade to try and pick out the suspects, but as at no time during the car-jacking was in a position facing any of them, I wasn't much help with that.

During my daily work, I was often asked to meet clients after hours because many working people could only manage the evenings for an appointment. So one cold winter evening, I arrived at a small block of flats that our company had managed for some time. A tenant had asked me to come and see her about buying the flat that she was presently living in. It was just beginning to get dark, and the lighting in the building was not very good. The streets in that area were not the best place to be in at night, so I parked right outside the building. As I climbed the stairs to get to the second floor, there were two young men coming down the stairs, and by chance, I happened to notice one of them was peering through the peak in his cap at me, thinking that I could not see his eyes. But they were fixed on my trouser pockets, presumably to see if I was carrying a cell phone or a thick wallet full of money. I carried on until I got to the lady's flat and knocked on the door. She opened quickly, and we stood talking in the corridor. At that point, the two men came back up the stairs and passed us while we chatted in the corridor. Again, I saw his eyes checking me out. They both had a very 'shifty look' about them, like a couple of 'Tsotis' (Zulu word for criminals). I soon realised they were probably going to wait until I was on my way out and try to mug me. I was feeling like a 'sitting duck' and needed to get the hell out of there. So after a brief chat, I left as quickly as I could, going back down the dark stairs, but I could hear footsteps coming from behind me now. This they must have thought was their moment, so I rushed down the steps four at a time and exited the building. I got onto my parked car as quick as I could, and as I drove off, I saw in my rear-view window the two of them looking around, confused and wondering where I had gone. These incidents felt like warnings of something bigger to come, and my fears only seemed to be enlarging the size of these problems. I needed to be more cautious in the future! Who was I trying to impress anyway? I guess it was my way of proving the 'freedom' I constantly sought.

This property boom did help restore some feelings of safety and also confidence in the property market; however, the city centre as a business capital never recovered, and most large corporations moved to the plush northern suburbs of Sandton and Randburg, where high-rise buildings began to pop up on the skyline. There are huge plush shopping centres now scattered around the outer city leafy affluent suburbs. Yet, the high-rise city centre is now, like most African cities, a hub of activity for street traders hustling and bustling their colourful wares, with music blaring out all around. Most of the old office blocks have now been converted into cheap residential apartments to try to ease the overcrowding. Some order has now returned, although it is a chaotic order that can cause much confusion to the un-expectant visitor. Just as most African cities have this hectic craziness about them that can be compelling to witness.

Chapter 13
Slums and Slumlords

One day soon after I had started in this company and desperate to make some commission because I was broke again after a recent divorce and urgently needing to pay my child maintenance and next month's rent and avoid being evicted, my boss had called me into his office. He said that he wanted me to go and see a client who was a regular buyer of rundown blocks of flats in the inner city. We had a building for sale that consisted of 12 flats that our company had managed for some time, but the tenants had now stopped paying the rent due to the bad state of the building. The owner was desperate to offload it as he had already fled the country because of the recent change in government after the collapse of the apartheid regime. Trevor Stone was the name of the prospective buyer, who my boss told me was a slumlord with plenty of disposable cash to buy at the right price, for him of course. A slumlord was a landlord who basically bought rundown properties for knock-down prices and rented them out to the low-income earners and then just collected the rents while doing nothing much to improve the living conditions or even maintain the building. These properties were usually overcrowded and many of the tenants were unemployed and often of a criminal persuasion. To collect the rent in cash, Trevor Stone would often have to come with a bodyguard, and it was believed that he even carried a gun. Most of his tenants, being low-income earners, paid in cash or they were self-employed hawkers and hustlers with no such thing as a bank account. In the days before bank cards were so easily available and when internet banking did not exist yet, the old-fashioned way of knocking on doors to collect the rent in cash was becoming a nightmare for landlords and their staff doing their collections. Muggings were on the rise, and even the staff who collecting rents were often in on the scam. I knew of a property owner with a few flats who employed a rent collector that absconded and disappeared at the end of his monthly collection with a few thousand rand in cash on him, presumably because the temptation was too great for an employee earning far less than what he found in his hands at the end of the month. So, I arranged to meet Trevor at this particular block of flats one afternoon. He turned up, not with a bodyguard nor a gun piece, but instead, a beautiful fancy piece, which was his latest girlfriend. He was about fifty years old, of average height with a stocky build and a barrel-like chest. He had a pair of dark sunglasses on, a thick gold chain around his neck, and this attractive oriental woman on his arm, who was half his age at least. He was very pleasant and friendly, though, as we toured around the building and into some of the flats. The tenants were reluctant to let us in and looked wary of us, probably sensing that their free accommodation was about to come to an end. The place was in a terrible state. I even noticed rats in the basement among all the rubbish strewn around the floor, but fortunately no one else seemed to notice because I managed to distract their attention. As we left the building Trevor Stone leaned towards me and said in a thick cockney accent, "fanks Georgie, but don't waste mi fuckin time bringing me to a dump like this." As I made my way back to the office I was astounded, because my boss had painted a different picture, making out this dingy block of flats would be just up his alley, 'excuse the pun'. I was down for the rest of the day. The following morning, I managed to put it behind me and pushed on to the next project. That's when I got a call from none other than Trevor Stone, who asked me to arrange a meeting as soon as possible with the seller of this rundown block, at our offices, as he wanted to put in an offer on the property. As soon as I put the phone down, I knew how stupid I had been. I should have realised what he was up to the previous day, making out he was not interested. It is one of the oldest tricks in the business and the clearest sign of an interested buyer. The prospective buyer will play down his interest and rubbish the property, making out that it's not for him, so as to try and get a knock-down price. How I didn't see this coming?

A couple of days later, we met in our boardroom with my boss present as he knew what to expect from his vast experience, as I was still a bit new to the game. My previous boss always used to say that the most important thing was, "Don't think for your clients." In other words, let events play out and don't try to control proceedings. Trevor Stone arrived by himself looking as suave as ever and soaked in at least half a bottle of 'Eau de Cologne', and the seller was there too, looking a little down and far too eager for my liking. As we all sat down to talk pleasantries and then haggle a little, Trevor Stone soon pulled out a chequebook and proposed to pay for the property there and then at a pretty low price, of course. At that point, everybody looked at the seller. A mere shadow of disquiet flitted across his bonhomie as he seemed to be recalling the past. In property negotiations, it is vital that you do not speak while the seller chews through this moment after a price has been mentioned. The silence was almost painful, and then he gave in and accepted. Trevor also wanted to take over the property the next day and get the tenants paying rent again straight away. He no doubt had his methods for getting money out of people, but that was not the concern of anyone else present. After some jostling and whingeing, the deal was drawn up and all parties signed the purchase agreement. The next day I got my commission paid out to me which saved me from being evicted, and I had enough money for the next few months while I continued selling. What was most astounding was that it was a most unorthodox way to sell a property as usually, as I mentioned previously, the payment to the seller and agents is the last of the transactions to occur, some months later and after all legalities and deeds having been transferred to the new buyer, and not the first thing as in this case. In all of my next ten years of selling property, it never happened again like that. I did have many other dealings with Trevor in the years to come, and he turned out to be a likeable rouge and certainly helped save the inner city from squatters and criminals that were taking over the decaying and abandoned buildings that were spreading through this once thriving metropolis.

Now that the apartheid laws had been scrapped under the new government, there were believed to have been well over one million newcomers flooded into the country and more coming, with a large percentage of them having descended onto the streets of Johannesburg since the eight years of independence. Many came from neighbouring countries like Zimbabwe, Zambia, Mozambique, and Angola. They mostly came over the borders illegally, without visas or work permits. Others came from the far reaches of Africa, like Nigeria, Ghana, Kenya, and Ethiopia, as the immigration department struggled to control the influx. Crime was now rampant in the city, and multi-storeyed buildings were being hijacked on a regular basis. Controlling a building was a lucrative business for the hijackers because the squatters who were recruited to fill them paid a minimal fee for sleeping on the concrete floors, often with no running water or electricity. There could be as many as a thousand people living in one ten-storey office block. With no sewage, the stench of excreta and the smoke from open fires was like a scene from the dark ages of plague and disease in the slums and workhouses of many European cities. Of course, this only added to the already growing crime wave that had taken over the city centre.

The government had eventually tried to combat this problem. They formed a large team of highly trained security guards, armed with truncheons and sjamboks, who would ascend on hijacked buildings, rushing the large office blocks and flushing out all the illegal occupants. They were named 'The Red Ants' because they wore bright red workmen's overalls with red construction helmets as they swarmed the area with tear gas and a no-nonsense aggression. They would do dawn raids on these targeted building, literally flushing out the whole building using brute force to clear the place of people and possessions, which were then piled high onto the streets. The building was then sealed off and guarded while the rightful owner could take back control of their now 'shell of a building'. This always created a mass crowd of onlookers who had gathered in the streets to watch this terrorising swarm of 'Red Ants' buzzing around. It would usually always make the news headlines too, with helicopters filming this spectacle from the air, which made it all the more impressive and 'ant-like'. To witness all this on mass was quite a spectacle and it was highly effective in the attempt to save the city from being overrun by mob rule, and now it had become a common feature of life in 21st-century Joburg. There was even a film made in Johannesburg in 2008 called Jerusalema'. It's all about the drug lords who controlled the inner-city slums and how they fought to take control of hijacked buildings as an easy way to make money from the poor and desperate due to the influx of people seeking out prosperity in the once-prohibited, now thriving areas of the city. It was not just the foreigners who flocked to the cities. During the apartheid years, even the rural black South Africans living in the homeland areas were denied access to the major cities. This was called the 'pass laws', which required all blacks, Indians, and mixed races to carry a 'pass' which stated which areas they were allowed to live in. This was to limit the influx of people into the cities and so the police had more control of crime and overcrowding. Now under the new government, movement was unrestricted and, as is the norm around the world, the upcoming generations seek the fast-paced, rat-race existence of city life and escape from the drudgery and snail pace of the rural village!

As more and more businesses moved out into the suburbs to get away, more buildings were becoming emptied and now vulnerable to illegal takeovers. Even the Johannesburg stock exchange moved and built new premises in the plush northern suburbs, which was now becoming the new business hub with huge shopping centres too. The 'big four' banks and the Johannesburg daily newspaper 'The Star' were about the only large private corporations to keep their head offices central and resist the trend of fleeing. But even they struggled to get the best staff, who were more likely to prefer working in a safer environment. The local municipality and government departments were of course expected to stay put, otherwise there would have been no confidence left in the future of the city already showing huge signs of urban decay. With the efforts of the 'Red Ants' and the extremely low property prices, there was a sort of revival taking place. The property developers had now seen an opportunity and snapped up these building that were now just a concrete shell, and they converted them into blocks of cheap, low-income housing. This started an upturn in the prospects of the inner city. Cameras were placed all around the city streets and many security guards were employed to try to combat the rising crime. The ruling ANC Party then occupied a whole office block as their headquarters, which appeared to be a good political gesture. If the unemployment rate and the influx of illegal immigrants could be reduced, it was likely that there could be a healthy revival in down town Johannesburg. Some of the great cities of America, i.e. Atlanta, survived the same downward spiral and have risen up from the rubble of the past, and it even hosted the Olympic games in recent times.

It did eventually help restore some safety and confidence in the property market in South Africa, however, the city centre as a business capital never recovered, and most large corporations moved to the plush northern suburbs of Sandton and Randburg, where high-rise buildings continued to pop up on the skyline over the next decade. Johannesburg had managed to stem the tide somewhat and even played host to the recent 2010 World Cup final, which went down with great success.

Chapter 14
Dark Night of the Soul

Having a tough time, depressed and confused, I bumped into Mr Lee again. He had a knack of turning up just at the appropriate time. We talked about some of the great men and women who have paved the way for humanity to evolve. He said that there always had to be a living messiah on earth; otherwise, the world might implode, and that would be the end of this particular epoch of time and space. He said there had been previous worlds created millions of years ago before this current one, but they had imploded and ceased to exist, and they had only lasted for very short times. There had been attempts that failed and collapsed shortly after coming into existence, and the residue of that dark energy still exists here and now with evil entities that inhabit our underworld and can enter the human psyche of those who have week and unstable minds. This world we are in now has been far more successful because there are people walking this planet right now who are every bit as enlightened as Krishna, Buddha, Mohamed, or Christ. Most of us would not even recognise a messiah even if we came face to face. "It takes one to recognise one," as the saying goes. He or she most probably wouldn't be wearing a robe and sandals, I suppose!

Mr Lee said that "whenever you are facing the dark night of the soul, that is a sure sign you are on the right path because these are also great moments of movement and growth. It could not be any other way, for heaven needed the strong and tested; otherwise, it would not serve the greater purpose. Of what use would you be in the higher worlds if you have not coped in the lower ones?"

The property market boomed for some time and I had a few prosperous years of relative stability, financially at least. Our company grew and moved into larger premises. Sales were increasing fast because the previously denied local black population were now offered the opportunity to buy property on 100% loans. Property developers could hardly keep up with the demand for new accommodation. We took on more sales agents and staff to cope with the demand. That is when Claire arrived to work in the administration department at the beginning of a new year. The day she arrived is still etched in my mind as we were introduced to each other, for I instinctively knew that it was a fated meeting of old souls. There was a recognition on some deep level even though we were complete strangers in that first moment we set eyes on each other in this incarnation. After a few months, I began to realise there was something going on. I could feel it, but I could not act on it. Intuition can feel very real but needs to be backed up with some solid proof. Timing is crucial, and before the time is right, it is never the right time. However, I had not anticipated what was to happen by the end of the year. It took some time, but we were eventually drawn into powerful romantic connection that was so intense I could not determine where I ended and where she began. It was the first relationship where I felt a free abandon. I realised this is the feeling that true love is supposed to be, without the ties that bind that eventually cut off the flow of energy that brought you together in the first place. My usual experience of love and romance was that it was either paradise or purgatory, swinging from high to low with some moments of bliss and some of confusion, wondering what the other person was feeling. Then, after the novelty period of a few months had passed, the relationship often turned into a power struggle with our home turning from a love nest into a battle ground. However, with Claire it was a new experience where we would sit and look into each other's eyes without shame and judgement. We seemed to be on the same level. It was as though she was a female version of me or the other half of me that made me whole. There was a total honesty without words. We made no promises. In fact, there is something pedantic and desperate about promises. They deny faith and spontaneity. Sometimes words were just not necessary. But I recalled the words of a Roy Orbison song that says, "If love is blind, then I don't want to see!" It certainly felt like I was stumbling into something that I could not even fathom what It was; that is the beauty of love. We were lost in each other. There were many times that I felt a telepathic connection with her, like our minds were one. The romance was like a beautiful dance where every moment was played out in perfect harmony. We were moving in step and the synchronicity was effortless. When you are in this flow, it feels like all your stars are all lined up and everything makes more sense. We lay together at times just exploring each other. I felt the deepness of her kisses on my lips, and I touched the wetness between her legs. When we made love, she took me to places I'd never been! Of course, I know that this is pretty much what all love affairs start off with, but for me, the intensity felt it was now multiplied by 10. Being together felt the most natural thing I had ever experienced, and parting for a few days left me with no anxiety or any desperation to be with her again soon. I felt like I had been freed. This love had released our inhibitions and vulnerability. Trust, without the need to control or be defensive. Some days, I just went for a long walk by myself and daydreamed of the time we had together, without the need to want her to be here in that moment. The future did not exist for us right now while we were stuck in the present moment. I was experiencing life in harmony because all aspects of my life were going well, or at least that's what it felt like. Yes, there were disappointments and the usual hiccups in life, but they were now less important. Are we not looking for the divine in a lover? Love is then the union with the god/goddess in the other. I instinctively knew that inevitably this relationship would eventually come to an end at some point because whatever has started will have an ending just like the universe itself. However, this feeling was not a dread because the love we had was unconditional and eternal and would last until all time. Just like the love for your child that never dies even when you are separated through time or distance.

Then, as predicted, the property bubble eventually burst in 2010, and all around the world, the property market went into a nosedive due to the reckless lending by the eager financial organisations. So, I saw tough few years ahead for sales and decided to move into letting and property repairs to make an easier living. It did provide a reasonable income, but it was not my cup of tea as I needed something more challenging and an opportunity to be more creative. But I stuck it out for a while, just biding my time until I was sure of which direction I was going to go in.

I had taken up painting portraits a few years ago, and so now I decided that I was painting some worthwhile portraits and decided to make a go of exhibiting and hopefully selling some paintings to make a reasonable living from being an artists, for this is what my passion had been from the early days of being at school. I knew many artists had failed miserably in the past, but I now had some business skills and good selling experience along with some artistic talent. It is said that many artists struggle because, "the artist is rarely a thinker and the thinker is rarely an artist." If I could balance these then maybe I could succeed in the present art world like so many more artists have done in recent times. So, I took the risk and plunged into another career change. I had some money now that would give me some time to get going. I soon found out that portraiture was not a popular subject matter at this moment in time. Gallery owners recommended I should paint landscapes or wild animals for the African tourist market! But I was not in it to succumb to the needs of others and ultimately, I was not in it to make a quick buck. Trying to separate the desire to make a living to feed myself and family along with the need to express myself fully and feed my soul was now a conflict that would cause a lot of anguish over the next few years. I kept on and on but nobody seemed to give a damn, and eventually, I learnt to overcome the indifference that I came across. I carried on regardless because alas, the artist is the eternal optimist. My relationship with Claire was also heading towards an ending and as with all things they have their time to grow and a time to wither and die. As expected, it ended amicably because we had few needy attachments to each other and the parting was our way of moving on in our own choice of directions.

When I spoke to Mr Lee about the confusion of my new career, he simply said, "Life will be very difficult for anyone who tries to raise a family without a regular source of income but more so for anyone who tries to raise a family without a soul." Again, the paradox of life was deep in my thoughts and making me contemplate and ponder a while. I pushed on and struggled through many months of rejections with my art. I had managed to sell very few paintings. However, I was now nearly broke, and on the brink of collapse. That's when I had a vivid dream.

I was crossing a bridge in the dead of night, hardly able to see where I was going. The strange thing was that I was climbing along the bridge from the outside hanging on to the steel structure and edging along. Then Nelson Mandela appeared alongside me and I looked up at him with his famous smile and he told me to 'just let go'. With that, I let go and that's when the dream ended. Trying to analyse the dream, it was very strange to me that I had chosen to cross the bridge from the most difficult position, instead of just crossing on top of the bridge. Was I doomed to a life of struggle or was an easier life still an option? Had I now developed a 'scarcity consciousness' where lack was constantly with me? My destiny was out of my control right now as letting go meant stepping aside and allowing my 'higher self' to be the more prominent, over my faltering ego.

In this short story by Hermann Hesse, the hero 'Klein' says, "Wonderful thoughts of a life without dread! To overcome dread, that is redemption! How he had suffered from dread all his life, and now, when death had him by the throat, he no longer felt it, no dread, no horror, only smiles, release, consent. He suddenly knew what dread was, and that it could be overcome only by the one who recognised it. He felt the dread of death above all. But in reality, all dreads were only masks and disguises. The truth was there was only one thing we dreaded, that of letting yourself fall, taking that step into uncertainty, the little step beyond all the securities that existed in you. And whoever had once surrendered themselves, and let go one single time and practised the great act of confidence and entrusted themselves to fate, was liberated. They no longer obeyed the laws on earth. That was it! It was so simple!" But letting go feels like 'suicide'. In the Koran it states, "Trust in God but don't forget to tie up your camel!"

If we could face up to what we are constantly turning away from and then by acknowledging it, it disappears. The answer would be to just stop!. To stop the continuous act of anxious thinking because it doesn't serve anyone. It's so simple and it leads to peace. Surely then if we had a little trust to let go of our constant clinging on, then we would begin to flow along with nature instead of struggling against it. Here is a short story by Richard Bach, in his book 'Illusions', that goes something like this.

The story of the Reluctant Messiah.

"Many years ago, there was a land up in the mountains, where a people lived in its fast-flowing rivers. They lived by clinging onto the rocks and shrubs, fearing they would be washed down by the rapid current and smashed against the rocks below, resulting in death. Then one day, there was a being who decided he was fed up with this constant clinging as a way of life. He felt there was more to his existence than just clinging. But when he told the others, they just laughed and laughed, saying that he would be washed down the river and smashed against the rocks and would die! Months went by, and still, he was frustrated from the constant clinging. Eventually, he plucked up the courage and let go! He was washed down the river and tumbled among the rocks, but soon he was washed into the vast ocean below. He was now free at last from this life of clinging. Many years later, he decided to return to visit his fellow clingers. They were amazed and proclaimed a 'miracle' and made a messiah out of him. They carried on clinging and worshipped him forever more. He became the reluctant hero and left in despair to go back to his life of freedom."

Basically, we have a built-in herd mentality seeking out comfort zones in which to cling onto. However, there are about 5 % of the population who have been described as the 'Outsiders'. These are the dreamers with a creative drive and eternal optimism and like 'Warriors', they fight their own battles as opposed to the remaining 95% of us who are the soldiers happy just taking orders. The Japanese in the 'prison of war' camps from the Second World War had recognised this. They believed there where only about 5% of the prisoners who they labelled as troublemakers and were likely to attempt to escape, so once they were recognised and singled out, they were separated and kept in high security, whereas the rest of the prisoners were left to roam around with a lot more freedom and made no attempt to escape. The outsiders are the restless ones who are driven to greater purpose and to seek salvation by fulfilling their destinies. They develop great trust in universe beyond the normal blind faith that religions try to instil, for this kind of faith is just another form of clinging.

This, I began to realise, was the freedom I had been searching for: freedom from the confines of the ego. Always having to protect itself from the fears that well up from time to time as we struggle through a lifetime of movement and progress in a society that often seems to inhibit us from finding our individuality to be our true selves because it threatens the status quo of the whole. Then, when you do go it alone and break free, life takes on a new meaning. You begin to find there is a greater purpose in the universe! I had to give up the fight for money and security to find out what liberation really was!

Chapter 15
Letting Go

I let go and gave up all my possessions, my flat, and all my paints and artwork. Now I only had the clothes on my back and a small backpack full of things. I was now one of the homeless or 'displaced' as they call them officially in South Africa. Damaged in some way by their past experiences but determined to survive, somehow? Most of them are dossers who have hit the streets because of alcoholism or drugs; some are just socially inept and cannot hold down a regular job, so prefer this life without commitments. But where do I fit in? Why do I even need to fit in? I feel very confused about this position I'm in and I'm struggling to accept it. Was it something I had to go through to find what I was looking for? Or was it just bad karma I had created? Or some of both! I remember shortly before I became homeless there was an intuitive feeling of calm and confidence that all would be all right. But the reality now was far removed from that arrogant assumption. Heading out into my first night on the streets was a disturbing experience that constantly made me question, 'is this really happening to me?' and also 'if they could see me now?' referring to my parents and family. I had told no one of my predicament because I was too ashamed and mostly because I was still in denial. It was a shock to my system and somehow I still believed that something very soon would come up. An opportunity that would be my saving grace like it had in previous times of fate. Alas, this time it was for real. My first night, I sat outside a popular shopping arcade, just watching the world go by, still in disbelief and to pass the time until nightfall. There, I got chatting to a young man called Mac, who looked like he could also be homeless as he was rough-looking with a gaunt face and asking passers-by for money. He was about 28 years old, handsome and well-spoken, but he walked with an uncomfortable hobble like a very old person. I learnt later this was what happens to drug addicts eventually, as their joints become damaged from the heavy drug use. Otherwise, he looked fairly clean and well mannered, but he had no shoes. When I asked him why he was barefooted. He explained that they were stolen the night before while he slept on a busy pavement in the city centre. I thought, 'how rich is that'! When you have virtually nothing then someone literally steals the clothes off your back. Of course, there is a passage in the Bible that explains: "Those that have, more shall be added. Those that have not, the little they have shall be taken from them." Well, now that parable seems to make sense. When you are down and poor, you are inviting negativity and scarcity, and when things are going well for you and you are in a positive mood, you are inviting prosperity. Furthermore, if we can have the 'belief' that we are rich, even if it is not so, then we will become prosperous. "Whatsoever you believe, so it is." We chatted a lot through the evening, and I could tell that Mac had an intelligent and curious aura about him, like he knew something! Like there was something more to life than just this physical existence.

So where had he gone wrong? I wanted to help him! I heard it said once that the drug addict or even the alcoholic is subconsciously searching for the God because the high that they gain from their habit is the closest they have come to the divine! The problem is they end up crashing back down to earth again and again. Well, I wanted to help him and tell him about my experiences and help him to give up his destructive drug addictions, but any expert in psychology knows perfectly well you cannot push or help someone to do something they haven't initiated themselves. Besides, health is like money, you have to spend it to appreciate it. But it does run dry! Bob Dylan wrote, "How many times must a man turn his head and pretend he just doesn't see." I suppose they are just not ready yet!

The night was long as I waited for quite to descend, so I could curl up somewhere safe and secluded to just be alone with my misery. But as I bedded down, another fear came up. I kept thinking of the words spoken by the man who had his shoes stolen while he slept on the pavement. I'm on the city streets now where crime is rife and although I may have little or nothing to steal, I'm still in a vulnerable position and defenceless while I lay down and rested. I felt like a wild animal that lives with the constant threat of attack by its predators. I was now the victim and feeling very scared having to sleep in the open without a roof over my head. I began to realise how much we take for granted when things are going well for us, and we even moan about the weather or other petty irritations. So, searching for a suitable patch to call my own for the night, I found a secluded place in a church yard under a canopy, protected from the rain. I rolled out my sleeping bag on the concrete floor. The stars were very bright as I lay there alone, feeling very small. But I couldn't sleep because of the discomfort of the rock-hard floor and worry of attack. Eventually, I must have dosed for a few moments because I had a lucid dream.

I'm lying in a concrete alley-way between two tall buildings, too scared to sleep because of the dangers from the outside world. Then a very large steel hand comes down from above and covers me in a protective embrace, and I sense a feeling of peace. With the worry now eased, I drop off to a deep sleep and wake in the early morning, well-rested and with the sun rising. Knowing I must move on before anyone arrives for work and spots me there because I instinctively know, if I am to return here again another night I need to be invisible and leave the place without a trace. However, one night, some weeks later, I did eventually get ejected from that safe sanctuary when the church caretaker came home drunk and angry on a weekend in the wee hours of the morning. He prodded me with his foot and told me to leave now or he would call the security guards. So I move along, and 'moving along all day' is very much what my life had become like now, as a casual drifter.

Over the next few days, I wander around by day searching for food and searching for some understanding of why I have ended up on the scrapheap of society. I know that when you become true to yourself, you naturally reach your true place in life. So, have I been deluding myself right up until now and living a high life far beyond my true level? Or maybe this really is karma for some of the deeds I have committed in the past.

One late evening in a plush suburb, I passed a busy street of little bistros and fancy restaurants where well-to-do couples were dining on the sidewalk under the moonlight on this warm evening. The sight and the smell of delicious food made me drool as I passed. Some of the diners stopped chatting to look over as I passed with my backpack and well-worn clothes. "Well, I have eaten outside before in places like Soho, St Tropes, and Hong Kong" of course, I never verbalised that! But I missed the good life at these moments as I ambled down the street, holding my hat in awkward reverence. If I hadn't known such a life of plenty I could've have lived with having so little!

Whatever! How can I possibly get out of this dilemma? I feel that my dignity is floundering, and I'm beginning to sink into self-pity like all the other hopeless cases who are now my close neighbours. Trying not to be aloof, I join in conversations because I know I'm no better than them. But gradually, as I follow the trail of fellow seekers towards the church handouts each day in different parts of the inner city, I begin to come across the odd drop-out who seems to have risen above his misery and found some dignity in their seemingly hopeless existence lived in this 'paved dungeon'. I even come across some people with joyful happiness and a wry sense of humour. They had an 'air of acceptance' about them that was refreshing, but it disturbed me to think that they seemed to be okay with their predicament. Then suddenly it hit me, I realised the secret of street life is 'dignity', and that could only come from accepting 'what is'. If I am ever to get a job and move off this life on the pavement, then I need to just be with what is and not beat myself up all the time or slip into the 'shame' that passers-by and most of society will have labelled me with. I still have a life that matters, and above all, I still have potential. After all, isn't that the most important thing we have? A baby is born with nothing and yet is full of potential. 'Eureka'! I'm now free, freer than I have ever been before, and it's this freedom I've sought all my adult life! "Freedom is not having what you want, it's wanting what you have!" I wanted to tell someone, but I could not tell just anyone because they would think I had gone mad. "Living on the streets with nothing and now proclaiming I've found the secret of life!" Oh no! Was I now losing the plot? Where was Mr Lee now that I needed him? Sadly, I realised I may never see him again because I didn't need him anymore. He always tried to tell me I had an inner guide who I could rely on whenever I needed. "Most of the time we don't progress because the comfort zones of our present life are so reassuring," Mr Lee would state. This was when I decided I was going to have to stop going to all the 'soup kitchens' that were scattered around Jo'burg and to stop following the lonesome trail of all the other tramps on their way to their 'daily bread' because it was becoming a habit that I was likely to get used to and once that happened I might just fall into a comfortable routine that was going to be difficult to get out of. Living off handouts was a 'path of least resistance' and a way to survive that beats starvation at any price. However, I now had to put my trust in the universe. I would miss the guys who were my companions in poverty and were often so happy with their cheerful playfulness and who helped make this vagrant existence bearable and dare I say it, acceptable. I began to avoid going to charity handouts because it was important if I was to rely on 'grace'. I again remembered the saying, "Charity should be a hand-up, not a handout." Well, I had had my 'hand ups' and now it was time to find a way to move on and out of this dilemma. It seems strange to see it as a comfort zone but that's exactly what it becomes for some, who prefer to exist under the radar and therefore take little responsibility for themselves in the tough world of individual survival and development. It can become a form of escape! However, I tried not to judge them because it takes a certain kind of character to carry on living under these conditions which few would have chosen and I had no idea of what kind of life they had led before 'landing on the pavement' and besides I had hit this lowest rung too.

First, I had to find my dignity and centre myself by feeling good 'within myself', by coming to terms with where I was at right now. So, I phoned my best friend Dennis and asked to meet him somewhere for coffee and I told him about my situation. He was horrified at first but like all true friends he was Ok. He even offered to put me up for a short while with his family, but I had to decline because I knew it would only delay my worst predicament and also put me in a position of being subservient because of the shameful dependency. I felt strong enough now to face up to my responsibility to see this through. Then I told my ex-wife. She was furious at first because it meant that I was not able to offer any financial support for our children. She also offered to put me up for a couple of nights which I did accept as it gave me a few days' break to be with my daughters and prepare myself for the rough road ahead. As I eventually headed out to face the future alone, I felt a surge of energy for a short while, just from knowing that I was on the 'right path' even though it looked like a cul-de-sac. Soon reality kicked in, and I became sad. However, I knew that I was going to have to use all my strength and concentration to keep reminding myself of who 'I' was. This is what the Buddhists meant by 'mindfulness'. I was quite fortunate because practising mindfulness requires that you 'slow down and let go' of the frantic lifestyle that I had always lived, so for now, I had time on my side. I had the whole day and each day to just be, in the present. I roamed around the suburbs like the 'wandering Jew' or George Fox the dissenter and founding leader of the 'Quakers', who in the seventeenth century trekked up and down the English countryside preaching in fields and often sleeping rough. Fox was shunned by many of the established church organisations for his beliefs, i.e., "that women have souls" and "that believers could follow their own inner guides rather than rely on a strict reading of scriptures that religions were insisting." With all this time, I began to contemplate the deeper meaning of life? Things like the purpose of evolution?

Hunger was now my main concern as I sometimes went for days with very little food. There were times when I was living off scraps that had been abandoned with the usual 'accompaniment of flies', and then there were times when I came across food that seemed to be strategically placed on a park bench or in a plastic bag on the roadside. It tasted so good it felt like manna from heaven! I thanked the 'universe' for such gifts that had fed me and kept me from too much discomfort. The thought of eating food from a dustbin was repulsive; however, there were times I was so hungry and broke that I had to block out any shame. The months passed, and time slipped away as autumn leaves fluttered by. In the early morning chill as the sun rose, melting the frosted grass and warming my stiff little fingers, I would set off on a new day and take myself along the suburbs, picking my way through the landscape like a wild animal trekking its way instinctively towards a fresh water-hole. These Journeys my ancestors had all been doing for thousands of years, yet here I was suddenly aware of this single journey on this particular day like it was the very first time. I felt like 'Adam', and God was looking down on me in this moment. I had a purpose in the greater universe! But on other days, I felt pulled in opposite directions, lost and going nowhere. There were days when I was biding my time, like I was waiting for 'something', but other days felt like I was biding my time waiting for nothing!

It reminded me of a story I had heard many years ago. The story starts off about a travelling man who wandered the country from city to city searching some meaning in life. He led a difficult life and was always on the edge of society, never really fitting in anywhere. Things turned worse when he was thrown into a dungeon, accused of a crime he hadn't committed. He was to be condemned to death the very next day, but staring through the bars of the cell at the beast that was to devour him, he saw God in the pattern of its spots. He knew then that he was not going to die, that life was eternal. This jolt had 'awakened' him from a search for meaning in what seemed like a futile world.

Here is a passage from a book called 'The Green Face' by Gustav Meyerink:

"For thousands of years and more, some men have learnt to understand the laws of nature and put it to their service. Happy are they who have understood the meaning of this labour, namely that the spiritual laws are the same as the physical laws only an octave higher, for they shall enjoy the fruits of their labour while the others continue to toil, their faces turned downwards to the earth."

The key to this power over spiritual nature has been rusty ever since the flood. The secret is wakefulness. To be awake is everything.

Man thinks he is awake, yet in truth he is asleep and dreaming. He is caught in a mesh he has woven himself and the more he struggles, the tighter the net, for they are going through life like cattle to the slaughter. Unknowing, uncaring, and unthinking.

The dreamers are the active ones among us. They are never idle, never rested, eaten up by the mad desire for prosperity. They are like the busy beetles that climb all the way up a pipe only to fall down the other side and then start again.

They think they are awake but in reality they are sleep walking in a dream that is predestined down to the last detail, and they have no power to influence at all. There were and still are a few among us, those that knew they were dreaming, pioneers who reached the gates behind which the eternally wakeful spirit is hidden. Visionaries like Goethe, Blake, and Kant.

. The dreamers are the over-educated, they have forgotten how to walk and do not have the courage to throw away the crutches they have inherited from their predecessors. To be awake is everything.

Be vigilant in everything you do and do not believe you are already awakened. No, you are asleep and dreaming!

Gather all your strength together and for one single moment imagine with every fibre of your body, 'now I am awake'.

It will not come with too much thinking. Just sink beneath the surface of your mind. Just sink beneath the surface of your mind. This is known as the first gate.

If you can do that, then this is the first step on the long road from slavery to omnipotence. It will give you the power over all your thoughts that torment you.

Read the sacred writings of the ancestors, and like a thread running through them is all the hidden teaching of wakefulness. You must ascend rung by rung into even brighter states of wakefulness. These higher states are unknown to the masses and are assumed to be legends, but the story of Troy was for centuries believed to be a legend until recently one man found the courage to dig. The first enemy on this road to awakening will be your own body. It will fight you 'till the first cock crows'. But if you can see through the material world of this crazy debris and rise above the dreamers, who think they are men and know not that they are sleeping Gods, then sleep will leave you too and the universe will be at your feet.

No longer will you be like the snivelling slave that awaits a cruel idol, to shower gifts upon you or chop off your head. There is, however, one comfort that will be denied you. The secure comfort of a faithful dog who knows he has a master whom he is privileged to serve. But ask yourself, would you, even now as you are, wish to exchange places with your dog? Anyone who has started on the road to wakefulness will keep coming back to earth on an inner journey which will permit you to continue your work. You will be born a 'genius'.

Chapter 16
Homeless, Not Hopeless

Now that I had let go and accepted my fate, I felt much cheerier and my energy levels increased. I even managed to sleep well in the cold frost of the night on a hard concrete pavement. Humans are incredibly adaptable, being able to survive in almost all the conditions on earth. There were softer places I could have slept, like the grass in a well-kept park or among the bushes on the wilder side of life. However, I soon learnt why the hardened, perennial drifters kept to the well-trodden paths. In this case, the city pavements. First of all, the grass gets soaking wet from the dew of the night, and secondly, the wild creepy crawlers that live in the bushes are everywhere. One day, I woke up with a whole army of earwigs that had crawled into my sleeping bag with me. Presumably, they were just seeking out the warmest spots. I was even woken up one night by a curious fox sniffing my feet.

Another time, I found a nice dry spot on a pavement outside some shops next to a group of street urchins who were bedding down for another night. I was welcomed by one of them to bed down beside him. At first, a hush descended on the place, and I felt lonely among the group. They seemed curious how a white man could have sunk to the same depths as them, but they soon carried on in their cheerful banter. "We all have the same colour of blood!" one of them commented. They were very friendly and offered me some of their bread. They fell asleep very quickly as I watched their innocent faces looking beautifully peaceful and their blankets moving gently to the rhythm of their breathing. Eventually, I slept after my nightly exercise of tossing and turning. However, at about 2 am that night, I found myself being nudged by a drunken man who kept repeating that I had taken his spot and angrily forced me to get up and move to a less suitable part of the crowded pavement. I thought there must be a joke in there somewhere? The joke was on me! I was surprised how territorial we can be, even when we have nothing much to protect. This period of life as a drifter felt like a deliberate sabotage, as it forced me to become more relaxed, tolerant and less puritanical.

Although I felt a lot better about myself lately, there were days that were downright miserable. Spring was now approaching fast, and warmer the weather was much welcomed, but with that came the seasonal rains. There is virtually no escape from the wet storms, as all dry places are either taken or prohibited to trespassers like me, as the streets are well patrolled by the vast army of security guards that patrol 24 hours a day to keep the city streets clean and safe. I did eventually 'master the art' of finding the best sleeping spots. Dead ends and dark alleys with a smell of stale urine were the most peaceful and undisturbed once the local bars had closed.

The next thing that was getting me down was the lack of hygiene and the smell of my unwashed clothes that I had been wearing day and night, week after week. I had managed to find a regular place in one of the modern shopping centres to freshen up and splash my face each morning. When I looked in the mirror, I hardly recognised my own face. It looked skeletal with sunken cheeks. Washing clothes in the rivers is about the only option unless you can get an old friend to put you up for a night here and there just to get a good clean up.

Having mastered the art of survival in the concrete jungle like any 'extreme adventurer' would have to do living in the wild. Yet, there was always at the back of my mind, a feeling that something good was going to come of this and it would change my life for the better. Really! I was surely lost in delusion again? But as the Monty Python song goes, "Always look on the bright side of life." This had now become my mantra as I faced each new day. This I sang when I was feeling cheerful or even to get me out of feeling low and dejected.

I had been on the streets about six months now, and somehow, I was surviving without money, living each day as it came. I refused to ask for money to avoid pity or resentment, which are both likely to have an adverse effect on me. I had ceased to worry so much about how I was going to survive and where I was going to get my next meal. I was not overly starved, although hunger was a constant feeling, but maybe that was how nature is supposed to be. Animals in the wild are driven by their hunger and their need to survive, and that's what keeps them vital. The threat of death makes them more aware compared to caged animals or even domesticated ones. I was always looking for these kinds of positives in all situations, and I did manage to see the lessons to be learnt here, but it was tough to maintain that attitude for long periods. Reality kept kicking in, and with that, a feeling of hopelessness and defeat would descend on me, which was difficult to escape when you have so much time on your hands to ponder. The days were long, and the chances of finding any kind of distraction from my fallen status were not easy. At around this time, I came across a famous novel written many centuries ago, called 'Pilgrim's Progress' by John Bunyan. It gave me a great source of inspiration. It's about a family man who finds himself in difficulties with lots of doubts about his position in life. After many financial struggles, he decides to leave his wife and children who are now destitute and sets off upon a long journey that takes him face to face with many personal issues to confront and different people who offer some of their insight. After some time, he seems to have solved his difficulties or at least has learnt some great lessons and so returns home where his wife, now seeing the changes, wishes to take the same journey.

Now that I was forced to live in the present with this nomadic life, I even began to developed a way of looking at things. The shape of the clouds, the sudden appearance of a bird, the odd angle at which someone wore their hat? Whatever the thing observed became significant like it was speaking to me. Actually, it wasn't that the things in themselves revealed anything; it was just that one could find a means of connection to the soul of the universe. Everything in the world began to make sense, like being in love, that heightens your perception. I could recognise fear immediately by the lowered voice and the gaze. Any danger was picked up by the look in the eyes or a feeling of unease. Animals, of course, pick up on these things naturally.

I now had time to concentrate on getting a job, even if it was something menial, so I could at least contribute to my children's needs. Then one day shortly afterwards, I came across a poster outside 'The Hospice' head office where they had a large clinic that cared for people in the last stages of terminal illness. There they were having an open day and inviting anyone in to come and find out more about what went on in their organisation. So, I wandered in, hopefully not looking too dishevelled from living rough.

There was plenty of free food laid out on tables and an information desk that explained about volunteering and what kind of help they needed. Among the various tasks they required was someone who was good at fundraising by phoning the general public asking for donations or asking people to participate in their various fundraising events that they had on a monthly basis. I was told they had one space left, with a desk, computer and a phone, and they would like someone to join their team asap. I told them I had worked as an estate agent for many years doing cold calling on clients to sell their properties. They were as enthusiastic as I was about giving it a try. Eventually, I started there, working part-time at raising money.

It was a voluntary job without a wage, but there was a warm office with hot coffee and toast available all day and some good company with lots of interaction and laughs too. It certainly beat wandering the streets all day long, struggling to find some purpose to continue. I turned up day after day and managed to keep my living status a secret or at least I think I did because nobody seemed to notice anything odd about me, like having the same clothes on most of the time and maybe the strange odour of living rough.

After 6 months with some good donations that I had achieved, I was put on 10% commission on all the money I brought in. It was not enough money to get a room to stay in but at least it was employment, so I still remained on the streets but I was able to send some money for my family. Then one day I hit the jackpot and got a R72,000 donation from a commercial bank, and with my 10%commission, I was able to put down a deposit on a rented room, and after one and a half years on the streets, I was now back in the land of the 'homefulness'. So moving on from my past shame, I now found myself at work but strangely still staring death right in the face. However, it was not my own death now but that of the terminally ill patients where I was now employed.

The Hospice clinic was the place where those who were terminally ill, had no hope of recovery and in their last stages of dying, they were given some solace and offered some dignity by the extremely compassionate staff who tried to make their last days on earth peaceful. I began to see the irony of now being on the other side of hopelessness and now being able to help those in need who were going through their final days between life and death. I remembered a saying from some of the books I had read that, 'once you learnt how to die, you then truly knew how to live'. I had read the 'Tibetan book of the Dead' and knew that the Buddhist valued death very highly. So I wanted to know what it was like to accept death because death it seemed was always something that happened to other people.

I frequented the clinic building next to our offices and mingled with some of the patients who were now in the final stages of their illness. The 'Hospice does not make any attempt to cure patients who have been admitted because most patients have come from hospitals who have basically given up any treatment. So the aim of a Hospice is to try and make the process of dying a bit less painful and with some dignity. Drugs like Morphine are available to them even though it is highly addictive, but with no hope of recovery, that is irrelevant. It was here that I learnt about the four stages of dying which is commonly known among psychologists. The first stage, after being told that you are terminally ill and only have a short time left is; 'denial', i.e., "Death only seems to happen to other people" and "I'm going to beat this thing, I'm not giving up."

Even though the doctors have given up, we are rarely able to surrender to the inevitable so quickly. Then once we see the writing on the wall, we then go into the next stage which is 'anger'. "How can this be happening to me?" and "It's so damn unfair." Soon the anger turns to the third stage of 'self-pity'. They feel shame and a sense of failure. Which is quite natural, as death is the opposite of life and looked upon as failure in the Western society at least. The final stage is acceptance, and once this occurs they seem to now be able to see the beauty of life, for without death, life cannot be fully appreciated in all its glory. This is the yin and yang principle again which is like two sides of the same coin, life and death. When I first saw someone in this stage I was amazed. It is quite visible in the aura and the composure of the patient. They look as if they have suddenly had an 'awakening', as if something wonderful is happening to them. There is a freedom and serenity in final acceptance of death, that the healthy living were so often denied.

It was no coincidence that I ended up at this place because I was beginning to feel like I was now living out my destiny, and again, this lesson of letting go was vital to my journey. Now that I had let go of trying to be in control of my life, it began to come to me that we are all born with a destiny but we often fail to see it because we have free choice to go with this destiny or not. We tend to ignore the 'path less travelled' and so often follow the easiest option and so may miss our true calling. This then leads to disharmony and eventually disillusionment. Of course, the option is always there to wake up and smell the roses.

However, the older we get, the tougher it is to change. You only have to look around the busy high streets and in pubs to see many old folk there, who look defeated by life and have missed their chance, at least in this incarnation. Opportunities are continually coming our way to wake up and be true to yourself, for the right action is always within you if only you can let go of your ego and your fears and act from this point of your 'truth'. This is the place of 'the higher self'. It does not mean we have to annihilate the ego or that fear will no longer be with us. The ego is essential but should step aside and be the dutiful servant to the powers of the higher self. Difficulties will still be present but should no longer hold you back once you have learnt to trust the universe.

Having said all this, I'm sure death is not something many would wish for. In my case, homelessness is not a life I would have a chosen willingly and it is a miserable existence whatever the reason you have succumbed to it. I would not wish it onto anybody, unless they saw it as some kind of adventure and it could do them some good, say, if you had been living in a toxic comfort zone or on somebody else's charity. It can actually have a positive side to it, as many have found 'themselves' through adversity and then letting go of all their stuff and shaking off a fear of this 'ultimate humiliation'. A crisis can bring you face to face with who you are, which often happens when all else is stripped away, revealing that 'all is still good'. Frugality is one thing; it enhances life, but continual poverty and struggle can deaden it.

Not long after my own spell of homelessness, I did meet a woman in her fifties called Janet. She was very well-spoken and told me she was living in her sports car or at times in her tent when she was able to find a suitable spot. She told me she had to flee from a toxic relationship she had with a man who was quite wealthy and paid for accommodation, food, etc., but for all that, he was controlling and psychologically abusive, which seemed to be a common trait in all her other relationships. So, to get out of this cycle, she chose to go it alone to rid herself of her dependency. To me, she looked quite at peace with herself and cheerful, but of course, she would often go on about the misery and hardship that now confronted her.

There is nothing so revealing as when you are stripped of all the things, and it makes you realise you have been living as somebody you are not. Depression is the primal hurt that often sets in when you are no longer deceived by the illusion of power over people and the power of material things, and the depression won't go away until you begin the search for reason. It often moves you into self-realisation that can free you from yourself!

Alan Watts, the philosopher, has written a book called 'The Wisdom of Insecurity', all about this very subject. He claims that, "man's quest for psychological security is creating so much anxiety and our insecurity is the result of so much striving to be secure and that ironically salvation and sanity come from the recognition that we have no way of saving ourselves." We are like the creatures clinging to the rocks, unwilling to risk the humiliation of defeat and failure when in reality, this could be the quickest way to salvation as a species. We were not made to merely survive in a world like animals. We have the potential to rise up like Gods on chariots of fire and live a superhuman existence in paradise or heaven on earth. But alas, as this is our 'earth school' and we are still limited like adolescence, each one of us striving to find a way to live with more freedom and greater consciousness, and each experience is another lesson on this long road as we continue to evolve towards the goal of 'Awakefulness'.